INFANT BAPTISM

AN

INVENTION OF MEN;

OR,

DR. BUSHNELL'S ARGUMENTS REVIEWED.

WITH ARTICLES ON

ORIGEN'S TESTIMONY RESPECTING THE BAPTISM OF CHILDREN, AND ON BAPTISM FOR THE DEAD.

BY

REV. IRAH CHASE, D.D.

Philadelphia:
AMERICAN BAPTIST PUBLICATION SOCIETY,
530 ARCH STREET.

PREFACE.

Not long since, the writer of the following pages was asked by a very intelligent and conscientious friend, what satisfactory reply could be made by a Baptist to certain representations in Dr. Bushnell's volume on *Christian Nurture.* The book was taken down from its place on the shelf; and a conversation ensued which led to the review here presented.

The subject discussed demands the serious attention of every one who would be a disciple of Christ. It is intimately connected with Christian truth and Christian duties.

The testimony of Origen respecting the baptism of children presents decisive evidence, to which only a brief reference is made in reviewing Dr. Bushnell's arguments. The article on *Baptism for the*

Dead, while aiming to explain an exceedingly difficult passage of Scripture, shows incidentally the practical importance and the duty of adhering to what our Saviour has instituted.

May the reader seek for the truth with earnestness; and, like Paul in the glow of his first love, say from the heart, *Lord, what wilt thou have me to do?*

NEWTON CENTRE, *November* 18*th*, 1863.

CONTENTS.

I.

CRGANIC CONNECTION.

II.

JEWISH PROSELYTE BAPTISM, AND THE CONVERSATION WITH NICODEMUS.

III.

A DEVELOPMENT SUBSEQUENT TO THE DAY OF PENTECOST.

IV.

THE RECEPTION OF YOUNG CHILDREN BY OUR LORD, AND APOSTOLIC AUTHORITY.

V.

EARLY CHURCH HISTORY.

VI.

INFANT BAPTISM AND INFANT COMMUNION.

VII.

INFANT BAPTISM AND INFANT CHURCH MEMBERSHIP

DR. BUSHNELL'S ARGUMENT FOR INFANT BAPTISM REVIEWED.

I.

ORGANIC CONNECTION.

DR. BUSHNELL, in his work on Christian Nurture, lays down the following proposition, namely: *That the child is to grow up a Christian, and never know himself as being otherwise.* This he immediately modifies by adding: "In other words, the aim, effort, and expectation should be, not, as is commonly assumed, that the child is to grow up in sin, to be converted after he comes to a mature age; but that he is to open on the world as one that is spiritually renewed, not remembering the time when he went through a technical experience, but seeming rather to have loved what is good from his earliest years." Exceptions he admits; and he proposes to speak of these in another connection, when they can be stated intelligibly.

After presenting several weighty considerations in support of his proposition, he proceeds thus: "If we narrowly examine the relation of parent and child, we shall not fail to discover something like a law of organic connection, as regards character, subsisting between them; such a connection as makes it easy to believe, and natural to expect, that the faith of the one will be propagated in the other. Perhaps I should rather say, such a connection as induces the conviction that the character of one is actually included in that of the other, as seed is formed in the capsule; and being there matured, by the nutriment derived from the stem, is gradually separated from it. It is a singular fact, that many believe substantially the same thing, in regard to evil character, but have no thought of any such possibility in regard to good. There has been much speculation, of late, as to whether a child is born in depravity or whether the depraved character is superinduced afterwards. But, like many other great questions, it determines much less than is commonly supposed; for, according to the most proper view of the subject, a child is really not born till he emerges from the infantile state, and never before that time can he be said to receive a separate and properly individual nature.

"The declarations of Scripture and the laws of physiology, I have already intimated, compel the belief that a child's nature is somehow depravated by descent from parents who are under the corrupting effects of sin. But this, taken as a question relating to the mere *punctum temporis*, or precise point of birth, is not a question of any so grave import as is generally supposed; for the child, after birth, is still within the matrix of parental life, and will be, more or less, for many years. And the parental life will be flowing into him all that time, just as naturally and by a law as truly organic, as when the sap of the trunk flows into a limb. We must not govern our thoughts, in such matters, by our eyes; and because the physical separation has taken place, conclude that no organic relation remains. Even the physical being of the child is dependent still for many months, in the matter of nutrition, on organic processes not in itself. Meantime, the mental being and character have scarcely begun to have a proper individual life. Will, in connection with conscience, is the basis of personality, or individuality; and these exist as yet only in their rudimental type, as when the form of a seed is beginning to be unfolded at the root of a flower.

"At first, the child is held as a mere passive lump in the arms, and he opens into conscious life under the soul of the parent, streaming into his eyes and ears, through the manners and tones of the nursery. The kind and degrees of passivity are gradually changed as life advances. A little farther on it is observed that a smile awakens a smile; any kind of sentiment or passion, playing in the face of the parent, wakens a responsive sentiment or passion. Irritation irritates, a frown withers, love expands a look congenial to itself, and why not holy love? Next, the ear is opened to the understanding of words; but what words the child shall hear, he cannot choose, and has as little capacity to select the sentiments that are poured into his soul. Farther on, the parents begin to govern him by appeals to will, expressed in commands; and whatever their requirement may be, he can as little withstand it, as the violet can cool the scorching sun, or the tattered leaf can tame the hurricane. Next they appoint his school, choose his books, regulate his company, decide what form of religion, and what religious opinions he shall be taught, by taking him to a church of their own selection. In all this they infringe upon no right of the child; they only fulfill an office which belongs to them. Their will and character are designed to be the matrix of the child's will and character. Meantime he approaches more and more closely, and by a gradual process, to the proper rank and responsibility of an individual creature, during all which process of separation, he is having their exercises and ways translated into him. Then at last he comes forth to act his part in such color of evil, and why not of good, as he has derived from them."

In these passages it will be perceived that the author begins by representing the relation of parent and child to be "something like a law of organic connection, as regards character, subsisting between them." And this he further defines by adding, "Such a connection as makes it easy to believe, and natural to expect, that the faith of the one will be propagated in the other." Thus far, as the word "propagated" is most frequently used in a figurative sense, the statement seems entitled to a ready admission. But in the very next sentence there is an important modification: "Perhaps I should rather say, such a connection as induces the conviction that the character of one is actually included in that of the other, as a seed is formed in a capsule; and being there matured, by a nutriment derived from the stem, is gradually separated from it."

Here we are taught, not merely that there is something *like* an organic connection, and that the faith of the parent comes easily to be the faith of the child, but also that the character of the child is actually included in that of the parent, as a seed is formed in the capsule, or seed vessel, of a plant. "According to the most proper view of the subject," it is soon added, "a child is really not born till he emerges from the infantile state." He "is still within the matrix [or formative womb] of the parental life, and will be, more or less, for many years. And the parental life will be flowing into him all that time, just as naturally, and by a law as truly organic, as when the sap of the trunk flows into a limb. . . . Whatever the requirement of parents may be, he can as little withstand it as the violet can cool the scorching sun, or the tattered leaf can tame the hurricane. . . . Their will and character are designed to be the matrix [or mould] of the child's will and character." On the 30th page it is stated that "The parent exercises himself in the child, playing his emotions and sentiments, and working a character in him by virtue of an organic power."

These representations remind us of what we heard, forty years ago, at New Lanark, in Scotland. The distinguished free-thinking philanthropist, Robert Owen, had invited several strangers, who were from America and from various parts of Europe, to breakfast with him and his family. At the table he took occasion to advocate some of his favorite theories. *We are all*, he said, *creatures of circumstances*. And, holding up his coffee cup, he added, *We are no more responsible for our characters than this cup is for its shape*.

Here was truth, but not the whole truth; and the true was so exaggerated, and so connected with error, as to mislead. Dr. Bushnell, certainly, would be as far as any man from adopting Mr. Owen's conclusion. But too often his statement is an exaggeration; and it tends to mystify what it was intended to illustrate. It can hardly fail to mislead many an honest inquirer; and it may have confused, in some measure, the ideas of the ingenious and acute author himself. If he means to say that, through the arrangements of Divine Providence, there subsists between the parent and the child such a connection as enables the parent to contribute much towards forming the religious character of the child, we have nothing to object. Such a connection is involved in the organization of the family; and it was kindly intended to be pre-eminently an instrument of benefit, inasmuch as parents are pre-eminently the natural guides and guardians of their children. But what in this matter is emphatically the case with parents is the case also with others, in proportion to their opportunities of exerting on the young a good influence in the formation of character. This Dr. Bushnell does not and cannot deny. He seems to admit it fully on the 31st page, where he says: "Certain it is that we are never, at any age, so independent as to be wholly out of the reach of organic laws which affect our character. All society is organic—the church, the state, the school, the family; and there is a spirit in each of these organisms, peculiar to itself, and more or less hostile, more or less favorable to religious character, and, to some extent at least, sovereign over the individual man. A very great share of the power in what is called a revival of religion, is organic power; nor is it any the less divine on that account. The child is only more within the power of organic laws than we all are. We possess only a mixed individuality all our life long. A pure, separate, individual man, living *wholly* within and from himself, is a mere fiction. No such person ever existed, or ever can."

After a statement so explicit, it may seem captious to make any objection. But it is not to this statement that we object, except that what was intended to be expressed by the word *organic* would have been more readily perceived, if it had been expressed by some other word, or by a circumlocution.

Presented in plain language, the fact is very manifest that every person is influenced more or less by others, whether the influence be exerted designedly or undesignedly, and whether it be received consciously or unconsciously. The great human family are so constituted, or, in other words, mankind are so organized, that it cannot be otherwise. And in the formation of character, the young especially, as we learn from observation, reason and Scripture, are likely to be, in the greatest measure, either benefitted or injured by those with whom they are connected.

Here, it seems to us, is a solid and sufficient basis for Christian education, and for the most earnest and impressive appeals that can be made to parents. Dr. Bushnell, however, it is probable, has in his mind the exaggerated part of his representation when he says (page 31): "This view of an organic connection subsisting between parent and child, lays a basis for notions of Christian education far different from those which now prevail, under the cover of a merely fictitious and mischievous individualism." On the 29th page he says: "The tendency of all our modern speculations is to an extreme individualism, and we carry our doctrines of free will so far as to make little or nothing of organic laws; not observing that character may be, to a great extent, only the free development of exercises previously wrought in us, or extended to us, when other wills had us within their sphere. All the Baptist theories of religion are based on this error. They assume, as a first truth, that no such thing is possible as an organic connection of character." And (page 39), "How can we ever attain to any right conception of organic duties until we discover the reality of organic powers and relations? And how can we hope to set ourselves in harmony with the Scriptures in regard to family nurture, or household baptism, or any other kindred subject, while our theories exclude or overlook precisely that which is the base of their teachings and appointments? This brings me to my last argument, which is drawn from infant or household baptism —a rite which supposes the fact of an organic connection of character between the parent and the child; a seal of faith in the parent, applied over to the child, on the ground of a presumption that his faith is wrapped up in the parent's faith; so that he is accounted a believer from the beginning. We must distinguish here between a fact and a presumption of fact. If you look upon a seed of wheat, it contains, in itself, presumptively, a thousand generations of wheat, though by reason of some fault in the cultivation, or some speck of diseased matter in itself, it may, in fact, never reproduce at all. So the Christian parent has, in his character, a germ, which has power, presumptively, to produce its like in his children, though by reason of some bad fault in itself, or possibly some outward hindrance in the church, or some providence of death, it may fail to do so. Thus it is that infant baptism becomes an appropriate rite. It sees the child in the parent, counts him presumptively a believer and a Christian, and, with the parent, baptizes him also."

From this passage it is evident that Dr. Bushnell would have us understand, by an organic connection of character between the parent and the child, such a connection as authorizes us to presume that the child's faith is wrapped up in the parent's faith; so that the child is to be accounted a believer from his earliest infancy. An ingenious assumption indeed! but one that contradicts the common sense of all mankind. To account a child in his earliest infancy to be a believer is to account him to be what everybody knows that he is not; and to baptize him as a believer is to baptize him as being what everybody knows that he is not. This consideration alone is sufficient to show that the proceeding is unwarrantable, and that the assumption ought not to be made. We shall soon have occasion to show, also, that it cannot be reconciled with the teachings of our Lord and of his apostles, and with the practice of their earliest successors.

In regard to the statement that, "All the Baptist theories of religion are based on the error" of "an extreme individualism," we think that the author is under an erroneous impression. There are two extremes, the one ascribing too much to the parent and too little to the child; and the other, too much to the child, and too little to the parent. We would avoid both of these extremes. We would have parents lay to heart their responsibilities; and we would have children remember that they, too, are responsible to God. We would have parents fulfill their duties according to their best light and ability; and we would have children fulfill theirs, in the loveliness of filial obedience, with a due regard to the will of the Lord. And, as they come to evince a Christian spirit, and to have a competent knowledge of the simple truths of Christianity, so as to receive baptism and the Lord's Supper understandingly and with spiritual benefit, we would have them baptized, professing their faith in the Saviour, and their earnest purpose to live as becomes his sincere and devoted disciples. In their early childhood we would have them, according to their capacities, receive all good impressions and influences, from earth and from heaven. We would have them led by alluring example and timely instruction to him who said, Suffer the little children to come unto me, and forbid them not. We would have them brought up in the nurture and admonition of the Lord; and we would look fervently and confidingly to him for his blessing upon them. We would have them, like Timothy, when he was a child, know and love "the Holy Scriptures, which are able to make wise unto salvation through faith which is in Christ Jesus." And thus we would have them (to use the language of our author himself) "pass out, by degrees, through a course of mixed agency, to a proper independency and self-possession."

Dr. Bushnell represents his views of Christian nurture to be "radically one with the ancient doctrine of baptism and regeneration, advanced by Christ, and accepted by the first Fathers." He adds, "We have much to say of baptismal regeneration as a great error, which undoubtedly it is, in the form in which it is held; but it is only a less hurtful error than some of us hold in denying it. . . . The regeneration is not actual, but only presumptive, and every thing depends upon the organic law of character pertaining between the parent and the child, the Church and the child, thus upon duty and holy living and gracious example. The child is too young to choose the rite for himself; but the parent, having him, as it were, in his own life, is allowed the confidence that his own faith and character will be reproduced in the child, and grow up in his growth, and that thus the propriety of the rite as a seal of faith will not be violated. In giving us this rite, on the grounds stated, God promises, in fact, on his part, to dispense that spiritual grace which is necessary to the fulfillment of its import." (pp. 46, 47.) "Now the true conception is, that baptism is applied to the child on the ground of its organic unity with the parents; imparting and pledging a grace to sanctify that unity, and make it good in the field of religion. By the supposition, however, the child still remains within the known laws of character in the house, to receive, under these, whatever good may reach him; not snatched away by an abrupt, fantastical, and therefore incredible grace. He is taken to be regenerate, not historically speaking but presumptively, on the ground of his known connection with the parent character, and the vine or church life, which is the life of that character. Perhaps I shall be understood more easily, if I say, that the child is *potentially* regenerate, being regarded as existing in connection with powers and causes that *contain* the fact, before time and separate from time. For when the fact appears historically, under the law of time, it is not more truly real, in a certain sense, than it was before. And then the grace conferred, being conferred by no casual act, but resting in the established laws of character, in the church and the house, is not lost by unfaithfulness, but remains and lingers still, though abused and weakened, to encourage new struggles. Thus it will be seen that the doctrine of organic unity I have been asserting, proves its theologic value, as a ready solvent for the rather perplexing difficulties of this difficult subject. Only one difficulty remains, namely, that so few can believe the doctrine." (pp. 116, 117.)

This "one difficulty" is not easily removed. It arises from the utter unreasonableness of the demand made on our credulity. Respecting Dr. Bushnell's theory, a candid and intelligent writer, Professor Curtis, of the University at Lewisburg, Pa., has remarked as follows: "It assumes always a conjunction of three things, no one of which can be shown to occur at all. 1. That the parent shall perfectly discharge his duty; 2. That the Church shall also perfectly do the same; and 3, That if both of these do thus, God will in every case not only save that child at last, but effectually call it in earliest infancy; so that it shall 'open on the world spiritually renewed.' . . . It takes for granted that in the case of *every* child baptized, the two former, or human conditions, will be perfectly fulfilled ; and then it further presumes that the third or divine result will not only eventually but immediately follow. This we think the very extreme of presuming." *

How can any man wonder that so few can believe the doctrine ? Besides Dr. Bushnell's theory requires us to believe that the child is to be baptized as a believer on the ground of its organic unity with the parents; that baptism imparts and pledges a grace to sanctify that unity, and make it good in the field of religion; that God has given us the rite of infant baptism; and that He has promised to bestow the spiritual grace necessary to the fulfillment of its import.

* See the Progress of Baptist Principles in the Last Hundred Years, p. 257.

II.

JEWISH PROSELYTE BAPTISM, AND THE CONVERSATION WITH NICODEMUS.

THE true idea of infant baptism, it is asserted on the 43d page, "is seen most evidently in the history of its establishment by Christ, in the third chapter of John." The argument is set forth thus: "The Jewish nation regarded other nations as unclean. Hence when a Gentile family wished to become Jewish citizens, they were baptized in token of cleansing. Then they were said to be re-born, or regenerated, so as to be accounted true descendants of Abraham. We use the term *naturalize*, that is, to *make natural born*, in the same sense. But Christ had come to set up a spiritual kingdom, the kingdom of heaven; and finding all men aliens, and spiritually unclean, he applies over the rite of baptism, which was familiar to the Jews ('art thou a master in Israel, and knowest not these things?') giving it a higher sense: 'Except a man be born of water *and of the Spirit*, he cannot enter the kingdom of heaven.' But the Gentile proselyte, according to the custom here described—here is the point of the argument—came with his family. They were all baptized together, young and old, all regenerated or naturalized together;

and therefore, in the new application made of the rite to signify spiritual cleansing and regeneration, it is understood, of course, that children are to come with their parents. To have excluded them would have been, to every Jewish mind, the height of absurdity. They could not have been excluded, without express exception; and no exception was made. Some have questioned whether proselyte baptism existed at this early age; but of this the third chapter of John is itself conclusive proof; for how else was baptism familiarly known to the Jews as connected with regeneration, —that is, civil regeneration?"

We reply: No one has yet proved that our Saviour, when he spoke of being born again, expected Nicodemus to have in his mind proselyte baptism and civil regeneration. We are aware of the assumption made by Mr. Wall in his *History of Infant Baptism*, and of the array of authorities which he has presented. But those authorities are not competent and reliable witnesses respecting what was customary previous to the Christian era.

Our Saviour incidentally, on a certain occasion, intimated the pains that had to be taken to make a proselyte. "Ye compass sea and land to make *one* proselyte." In the depressed state of the Jewish nation, under the Romans, cases of proselytism, it is obvious, must have been much less frequent than at some former periods. Among those, however, which did occur within a few years of our Lord's entering on his public ministry, one was very remarkable. It was the case of Izates, king of Adiabene, a Syrian territory south of Damascus. The Jewish historian Josephus, a contemporary of the apostles, has given a particular account of this distinguished individual's becoming a proselyte and of his being circumcised; but he says not one word of his being baptized.* At a somewhat earlier period the Idumeans had, in effect, been compelled to adopt the Jewish religion. Josephus mentions their being circumcised, but of their being baptized in connection with their becoming proselytes he says nothing.†

De Wette, in his Hebrew and Jewish Archæology, says: "According to the Rabbis, circumcision, an offering and baptism were necessary to the reception of proselytes. Baptism, however, is probably a later institute, for it is not mentioned in the older writings, but only in the Gemara, whose testimony speaks merely for the time after the destruction of Jerusalem, and in other later writings. Yet, connected with proselyte consecration, there may have been in ancient times a kind of lustration, from which proselyte baptism (perhaps not without an intimation of the Christian) has risen.‡ Dr. Bengel, Professor and Superintendent of the Theological Seminary at Tübingen, says: "It was reckoned in the same class with all those other lustrations to which the Jews were accustomed. . . . It was not regarded as a *prin-*

* Antiquities of the Jews, B.XX.—C. ii. § 3 and 4.

† Antiquities, B. XIII. ix. § 1.

‡ Lehrbuch der hebräisch-judischen Archaologie, § 246, a.

cipal thing, nor as an essentially necessary part of proselyte consecration. . . . But the entirely changed condition to which they found themselves reduced by the overthrow of their state and of their temple" (A.D. 70) "led at length, as it seems, to new and finally more fixed decrees and regulations on this subject." (See his work on the age of the Jewish Proselyte Baptism, p. 115.)

According to one of the regulations, "a male is not baptized till he is well healed of the wound occasioned by the circumcision, *which always precedes.** Hence it is evident that proselyte baptism was not immediately connected with circumcision. It intervened at a considerable distance between this and the presentation of an offering, and was more closely connected with the offering than with the circumcision—which, strictly speaking, must always have been the *initiatory* rite, whenever it could be performed. After the destruction of the temple, the offering could not lawfully be presented; and after the destruction of the temple, also, there were times in which the Jews were by imperial authority forbidden to perform the circumcision. In these circumstances, the ablution would naturally assume a greater importance than at any former period.

Whatever may have been the time when proselyte

* Masculus non baptizatur, nisi vulnus culo illo, quod e circumcisione, *quae semper praecedit*, ceperat, bene curato. See Danzii Baptism. Proselyt, in Meuschen Nov. Test. ex Talmude antiq. Heb. Illustratum, p. 283.

baptism, ablution, or lustration first came into use, it was never performed on a proselyte's child born after the time of proselytism. How then could it be a model for infant baptism in regard to the children of Christians born after the conversion of their parents? Besides, the act was performed by the proselyte himself. John's baptism was administered by John to his disciples; and hence he was denominated the Baptist—that is, the Baptizer.

The ablution of proselytes among the Jews, whenever it was practiced, must, so far as it was initiatory, have had reference mainly to ideas of national purity on the one hand, or to a want of it on the other. The rite performed by the harbinger of Christ was not a national but a personal concern. It was administered to such Jews themselves as were penitent; and it had reference to the penitent individual's being cleansed from the pollution of his sins, in connection with the coming of the Messiah. Its import as a symbol of purification was readily comprehended in view of the addresses made to the people, and of its resemblance to the many ablutions to which they had been accustomed, especially whenever a person was cleansed from ceremonial defilements. This was always a personal transaction; and these ablutions were ten thousand times more frequent than any connected with the reception of the proselytes.

Dr. Bengel, in his work already mentioned, observes (p. 63): "John must have considered the question, *Why baptizest thou?* as referring to *his* baptism—to the essential and characteristic nature of it, already well known, on account of which the Jews believed that it would be committed only to the Messiah, or to one of his prophetic heralds. It was perfectly obvious that they who came with the question had reference to *his* baptism, which was so peculiar, that there should belong to it an altogether special divine authority. It would have been quite superfluous for them to have made particular mention of *proselyte baptism, which would not have been at all thought of in connection with John's baptism.*"

The whole subject has been re-examined by another German author, Dr. Schneckenburger; and he gives, as the result of his investigations, the following general propositions:

"1. The representation of the Talmud, by itself and in comparison with other accounts, cannot prove that proselyte baptism was established before the time of Christ.

"2. The passages from earlier writings, brought for the support of the Talmudical accounts, cannot afford any probable evidence, and much less, any certainty.

"3. The internal opposing evidence, furnished by the silence of the most considerable writers, or by particular facts which they have mentioned, retains its validity.

"4. The difficulties in the way of admitting that this custom came to prevail among the Jews after it had arisen among the Christians are not very great. Indeed, there are many reasons making it highly probable that, as an integral part of the initiatory ceremonies, it came up in this later time, as well as definite testimonies in favor of such an opinion.

"5. We are not, therefore, to think of deriving John's and the Christian rite from the Jewish one; and usages present themselves more akin to that rite, both in form and signification, than the ablution of Jewish proselytes appears to have been."*

To us, indeed, the assumption seems exceedingly improbable that our Saviour, in his interview with Nicodemus, had in his own mind, as the type, illustration, and model of entrance into his holy kingdom, any process of proselytism, vaunted and desecrated by Pharisaical formalists. On one occasion he says: "Woe unto you, Scribes and Pharisees, hypocrites! for ye compass sea and land to make one proselyte; and when he is made, ye make him two-fold more the child of hell than yourselves."† How much more reasonable it is to believe that in the case before us, he had in his mind the preaching and baptism of his harbinger, whose mission it was to make ready a people prepared for the Lord.‡ Nicodemus, with all his amiable courtesy, was a Pharisee. John had said to many of the Pharisees and Sadducees, "Bring forth fruits meet for repentance, and think not to say

* See the volume on the age of the Jewish proselyte Baptism and its connection with John's and the Christian Rite. Ueber das Alter der judischen Proselyten-Taufe und deren Zusammenhang mit dem johanneischen und Christlichen Ritus.

† Matt. xxiii: 15. ‡ Luke i: 17

within yourselves, We have Abraham to our father" (as much as to say, Expect not to be received as being the offspring even of Abraham); "for I say unto you that God is able of these stones to raise up children unto Abraham."* The burden of his preaching was, Repent ye; for the kingdom of heaven is at hand.† "The people that heard him, and the publicans, justified God, being baptized with the baptism of John. But the Pharisees and lawyers rejected the counsel of God against themselves, being not baptized of him."‡ Nicodemus might well be reminded of the inexcusableness of that rejection. The Messiah himself, it is well known, approved and vindicated the teachings and claims of John. The harbinger's preaching accorded with his own. Matthew (iv: 17) says: "Jesus began to preach, and to say, Repent; for the kingdom of heaven is at hand." And Mark (i: 14, 15) asserts the same, with some amplification: "After that John was put in prison, Jesus came into Galilee, preaching the gospel of the kingdom of God, and saying, The time is fulfilled, and the kingdom of God is at hand: repent ye, and believe the Gospel."

To repent was to have such a change of disposition as to loathe and forsake sin. It was equivalent to having a new heart, a heart to obey God as his dutiful child, and thus it was, in effect, to be born again. It was to be *taught of the Lord*, and led by his Spirit, so as to have a right spirit, an earnest

*Matt. iii: 8, 9. †Matt. iii: 2. ‡Luke vii: 29, 30.

desire to be cleansed from all sin, internal as well as external. In a word, it was to be prepared to enter, with humility and gratitude, the predicted kingdom of the holy Messiah.

Ought not Nicodemus, a teacher in Israel, to have known these things, and to have understood the expressions used by our Lord? Had he never read in the ancient Hebrew Scriptures, the prayer of a penitent, "Create in me a clean heart, O God, and renew a right spirit within me. Cast me not away from thy presence, and take not thy Holy Spirit from me."* Had he never read in the Prophets, Wash ye, make you clean; put away the evil of your doings from before mine eyes.† Repent, and turn yourselves from all your transgressions; so iniquity shall not be your ruin. Cast away from you all your transgressions, whereby you have transgressed, and make you a new heart and a new spirit; for why will ye die, O House of Israel?‡ A new heart also will I give you, and a new spirit will I put within you. . . . . I will put my spirit within you, and cause you to walk in my statutes.§ There shall come forth a rod out of the stem of Jesse, and a branch shall grow out of his roots. . . . He shall not judge after the sight of his eyes, neither reprove after the hearing of his ears. But with righteousness shall he judge the poor, and reprove with equity for the meek of the earth: and he shall smite the earth with the

* Ps. li: 10, 11. † Is. i: 16. ‡ Ezek. xviii: 30, 31.
§ Ezek. xxxvi; 26, 27.

rod of his mouth, and with the breath of his lips shall he slay the wicked.* All we like sheep have gone astray; we have turned every one to his own way: and the Lord hath laid on him the iniquity of us all.† Behold, I will send my messenger, and he shall prepare the way before me: and the Lord whom ye seek shall suddenly come to his temple, even the messenger of the covenant, whom ye delight in: behold, he shall come, saith the Lord of hosts. But who may abide the day of his coming? and who shall stand when he appeareth? for he is like a refiner's fire, and like fuller's soap.‡

Had Nicodemus duly considered such passages as these, he could not have failed to perceive, when our Lord spoke of being born again, that he had reference to that change of mind, that purification of the soul, which is involved in genuine repentance. It was manifestly a suitable preparation for entering the kingdom of that Holy One who could not be deceived, and who was to be to all "like a refiner's fire." Some of the Jews, it is certain, had substantially correct views on this subject. The preaching of John, and the baptism which he had been divinely authorized to administer, had made a deep impression, and awakened the minds of many. The statement given by Josephus, as well as the more ample record in the New Testament, is worthy of being remembered. He says, "Herod slew John that was called the Baptist, who was a good man; and who commanded

* Is. xi: 1. 3, 4. † Is. liii: 6. ‡ Mal. iii: 1, 2.

the Jews to exercise virtue, both as to righteousness towards one another, and piety towards God, and so to come to baptism; for that the washing with water would be acceptable to him, if they made use of it not in order to the putting away of some sins only, but for the purification of the body; *supposing still that the soul was purified before by righteousness.*"* Such a purifying of the soul, it is here evident, was understood to be distinct from the washing with water; for it was to precede that washing. The internal change was pre-supposed, as leading to the external acknowledgment, and as being requisite in order to make this a baptism acceptable to God.

There is a Rabbinic passage quoted by Schoettgen in his *Hebrew and Talmudical Hours*, according to which *He who repents of his sins is like a child born to-day.*† And on a memorable public occasion, our Lord declared, Verily I say unto you, Whosoever receiveth not the kingdom of God as a little child, shall not enter therein.‡ He knew what was needed, a state of mind childlike and humble before God. Who does not remember those impressive words of his: "Thou hast hid these things from the wise and prudent, and hast revealed them unto babes. Even so, Father, for so it seemed good in thy sight." And who does not perceive that, when he was conversing with Nicodemus, he was expostulating with

* Antiq. B. XVIII., c. v. § 2.

† Vol. 1, p. 328, from Ir. Gibborim, fol. 19, 3.

‡ Mark x: 15.

a person in danger of being blinded by Pharisaical prepossessions, and was teaching him what he most needed to learn ?

In every age, the grateful penitent has readily ascribed his change to God, the Holy Spirit. And *as many as are led by the Spirit of God, they are children of God.* They are born again, born of God, regenerated. These and similar expressions, all must admit, were used in the earliest days of Christianity for indicating the internal and moral change, the spiritual regeneration, which it demanded. They occur frequently in the New Testament, and sometimes in the early ecclesiastical fathers, as Justin Martyr, and Clement of Alexandria, though, at a very early period, baptism was often confounded with spiritual regeneration ; the sign, with the thing signified.

But in the case before us there is no room for such a confounding. Our Lord gives unmistakable prominence to the spiritual renewing. On this he expatiates, as the great absorbing subject ; and he finishes his illustration by saying, " So is every one that is born of the Spirit." Then, in words of mingled tenderness and dignity, he proceeds to press on the Pharisee's conscience the neglect of ample evidence, and to set forth the great object of his own coming into the world, that whosoever believeth in him should not perish, but have eternal life ; the love of God in sending him, and the condemnation of men for loving darkness rather than light, because their deeds are evil. Common sense and common candor must understand him as speaking to Nicodemus, not of unconscious babes, but of responsible moral agents. So when he said to his apostles, "Go ye into all the world, and preach the gospel to every creature: He that believeth, and is baptized, shall be saved; but he that believeth not shall be condemned." He had reference, most manifestly, not to unconscious babes, but to persons to whom the gospel could be preached. We need not doubt that what we cannot do, he, the wise and compassionate Saviour, will provide for the little ones, in a way adapted to their state.

According to the great commission, he that trusts in the Saviour and obeys him (for baptism is the appointed manifestation of a purpose to obey him in all things) shall be saved. But he that refuses to trust in him shall be condemned.* The unbeliever is

---

* If any one is troubled that in referring to Mark xvi: 16, we have written *condemned* for damned, he will, we trust, have his mind relieved by the following considerations:

1. *Condemned* expresses truly and exactly the sense of the word in the Greek original.

2. In the latter part of the conversation with Nicodemus, condemned is used as the opposite of saved; and condemnation as the opposite of eternal life; and, in referring to Mark xvi: 16, it was desirable to use the word *condemned* instead of damned, in order to bring out more clearly the parallel between the two passages.

3. In 1 Cor. xi: 31, the apostle Paul says: "We are chastened of the Lord, that we should not be *condemned* with the world."

to be condemned for his unbelief, his sinful neglect of the gospel. In his case, baptism is not mentioned at all. It is precluded by his unbelief. So, in the latter part of the conversation with Nicodemus, it is declared that the believer has eternal life ; but that the unbeliever is condemned for his unbelief, because he loves darkness, and perversely refuses to come to the light. In his case, also, baptism is not mentioned at all, it being precluded by his impenitent and sinful unbelief.

---

4. In John v : 24, condemnation is mentioned as the opposite of everlasting life ; and the Greek word, which is here translated condemnation, is, in the 29th verse, translated damnation. But, manifestly, the meaning would have been the same had the passage read thus : The hour is coming in which all that are in the graves shall hear his voice, and shall come forth ; they that have done good, unto the resurrection of life, and they that have done evil, unto the resurrection of *condemnation.*

5. In the sight of God, condemnation rests already on impenitent and unbelieving sinners here, and it must also be met in the future world, when the final sentence is pronounced by the righteous Judge.

6. When, in view of the scriptural usage, mention is made of sinners as being condemned of God, we naturally think, not merely of their present condemnation, but also and especially of that which awaits them on the great day of future judgment ; so that no advantage whatever is given to those who deny what was so impressively taught by our Saviour.

7. We need much wisdom and grace to enable us to present unwelcome truths faithfully and beneficially to the minds of our fellow-men. The preacher sought to

Surely, we can discover here no traces of Jewish proselytism, and no evidence of our Lord's establishing Infant Baptism. On the contrary, we have seen that he taught in harmony with John, whose teaching

---

find out acceptable words, and that which was written was upright, even words of truth. (Eccles. xii : 10.) We must all appear before the judgment seat of Christ, that every one may receive the things done in his body according to that he hath done, whether it be good or bad. Knowing, therefore, the terror of the Lord, we persuade men. (2 Cor: v. 10, 11.)

8. Dr. Doddridge, in his Family Expositor, has given the following translation and paraphrase of Mark xvi : 16. The translation, it will be perceived, is printed in italics: "*He who* sincerely *believes* your testimony, *and,* in token of that cordial faith, *is baptized* in my name, and continues to maintain a temper and conduct suitable to that engagement, *shall* certainly *be saved* with complete and everlasting salvation; *but he who believeth not* this my gospel, when opened with such convincing evidence, and finally persists in willful impenitence and unbelief, as he rejects the most gracious counsel of God for his recovery, *shall be condemned* by his righteous judgment to future and everlasting punishment, and shall, to his dreadful experience, find that gospel which he has despised to be a savor of death to him."

9. It will be seen that we have had reasons for using the word *condemned.* We should be very sorry to grieve or embarrass in the least any faithful minister of the gospel. We would gladly encourage and help him in his efforts to win the erring and sinful to Christian truth, to holiness, and to eternal life. *O that they were wise, that they understood this, that they would consider their latter end!*

and baptism had awakened much attention, and were exceedingly prominent in the view of the Jews. John's was the baptism of repentance for the remission of sins; and he, according to the best light then bestowed, directed to the coming Messiah those whom he baptized, saying unto the people that they should believe on Him who should come after him, that is on Christ Jesus.* The baptism which he administered presupposed repentance, a purification of soul, in the baptized. It had reference to one's own spiritual state and his purpose. It was thus a personal transaction. In this respect, it resembled the numerous purifications for ceremonial defilement among the Jews, and was easily understood, when administered to the penitent desiring to be purified from the defilement of sin.

Of the same character, unquestionably, was the baptism administered by the disciples of Christ, under his own eye, before his crucifixion. They were carrying forward the work begun by him who had baptized them, and whose ministry was "the beginning of the gospel of Jesus Christ." And when at last they were commanded to go into all the world, and preach, and baptize into the name of the Father, and of the Son, and of the Holy Spirit, they would not only from the terms of the commission, but also from the practice to which they had been accustomed, understand, that they were to baptize, not unconscious infants but penitent believers. The practice to which they had been

* Acts xix: 4.

accustomed is clear and undeniable. That of proselyte-baptism, it is probable, had not yet been established as a part of the ceremony initiating into Judaism. If it existed at all, it was of comparatively rare occurrence, and more closely connected with the presentation of an offering than with the circumcision, which alone, as the initiatory rite, was prescribed by the Mosaic law. The practice to which the apostles had been accustomed, it is well known, had the sanction of our Lord, but this cannot be said of any Jewish proselyte-baptism, or of its being transferred to the Christian dispensation, whether we regard the principle which it would involve, or the spirit which it would cherish.

The baptism introduced by John for penitent Jews, and practiced also by the disciples of Christ before his crucifixion, and not any Pharisaical ablution of a proselyte, would be the baptism of which these disciples would think, when they received the final commission, modified only by the more full declaration which our ascending Lord saw fit then to make. This was the baptism which they had reason to believe was "from heaven;" and it was associated with announcements and events proclaiming the Messiah and the establishment of the new dispensation.

The important fact to which we here call attention, ought not to be overlooked; and it cannot be frittered away by the groundless assertion that John baptized infants. Of this we have never seen a particle of evidence. That he did any such thing is contradicted by every intimation in the sacred record respecting his practice, and by the testimony of the Jewish historian, who speaks of him as representing his baptism to be acceptable to God, when received by the thoroughly penitent, *supposing still that the soul was purified before by righteousness.*

III.

THE SUPPOSITION THAT ON THE DAY OF PENTECOST, THE APOSTLE PETER PROCLAIMED AN INSTITUTE WHICH HE HIMSELF DID NOT THEN EVEN THINK OF, BUT WHICH, AT A LATER PERIOD, WAS PROPERLY DEVELOPED.

SOME who have been constrained to admit that in the New Testament there is no evidence for infant baptism, and yet have desired to retain the practice, suppose it to have been developed, some time after the days of the Apostles, from a truly Christian principle. According to their view, the good seed was planted; but at least one or two ages were required for its germinating into light, and yielding blossoms and fruit. Or, it was wisely kept out of sight; for, had it appeared earlier, it would have been assailed by the Apostle Paul, as being inconsistent with his great and favorite doctrine of justification by faith. Dr. Bushnell has his own way of viewing the matter. Without relinquishing arguments from the New Testament, he provides a scheme of development for saving infant baptism. From the words in Acts ii: 39. (The promise is unto you and to your children, and to all that are afar off, even as many as the Lord our God shall call), he gives a discourse entitled, *Infant Baptism: how developed.*

The apostle Peter, in the preceding part of his address, it will be recollected, had mentioned the promise in the prophet Joel respecting the gift of the Spirit, through whose efficacy the people, old and young, were to be moved and enabled to see visions and to prophesy.* And he had just said, "Repent, and be baptized every one of you in the name of Jesus Christ for the remission of sins, and ye shall receive the gift of the Holy Spirit." He adds immediately, " For the promise [respecting that gift] is unto you and to your children, and to all that are afar off, even as many as the Lord our God shall call." In other words, The blessings promised are for all that obey the gospel, whether old or young, at Jerusalem or elsewhere.

Such is the obvious meaning of the apostle. If any one doubts it, let him read the words quoted from the prophet, in the part of the address (Acts ii : 17) to which we have referred.

But according to Dr. Bushnell's explanation of the text, it is " a declaration that can signify nothing but the engagement of Christ, in his new and more spiritual economy, to identify children with their parents, even as they had been identified in the coarser provisions of the old. 'To you and to your children,' says the apostle; and here covertly as it were to himself, are hid infant baptism, infant church relations, potentially present but as yet undeveloped, even in what may be fitly called the seed sermon of

* Joel ii : 28. 39.

the Christian Church. This was no time to be thinking of infants, or children, as related to church polity; probably there is not one present in the great assembly. It will be soon enough to settle the church position of children, when the question rises practically afterwards. These converted pilgrims, Parthians, Medes, Elamites, and strangers of all names, may not even so much as think of the question till they reach their homes again. But the language we can see is Jewish ; language of promise, or covenant, only with a Christian addition—'and to them that are afar off, even as many as the Lord our God shall call'—and Peter, as we know, did not really come into the meaning of this language himself till years after, when the great sheet let down from heaven three times, and the actual ministering to a Gentile convert, showed him whither, and how far, the call of the Lord might be going, in these times, to run. Let it not surprise us, then, that the facts of infant baptism, and of infant church relations, covered as they are by Peter's language in this first sermon, are still not yet developed, even to himself—any more than the fact of Christ's call to the Gentiles."

But Christ had clearly commanded the apostles to go into all the world and preach to all ; and the prophets had foretold the conversion of the Gentiles. Peter and the other apostles needed to have the command brought vividly to their remembrance, with some additional instructions in regard to the time and manner of carrying it into execution ; but they must have known the fact that the gospel was designed for all.

Dr. Bushnell proceeds: "And when our Baptist brethren reiterate the formula, 'believe and be baptized,' 'believe and be baptized,' which they assume to be absolutely conclusive and final on the question of infant baptism, because infants can not believe, they have only to make due allowance for the fact that Christianity must needs make its chief address at the outset to adult persons, and their argument vanishes. Christianity will of course address itself to the subjects addressed; and, telling them what they must do to be saved, it will not of course tell them, at the same breath, every thing else that is fit to be known. In this manner its language was naturally shaped, for a considerable time, so as to meet only the conditions of adult minds. When at length it shall begin to be inquired, What is the condition of immature, or infant minds? it will be soon enough to say something appropriate to them."

The language of Christianity, for a considerable time, it is here said, was shaped "so as to meet only the conditions of adult minds." If this means that the gospel addressed itself to those who were sufficiently mature to receive it, and taught them, first of all, what they must do to be saved, we make no objection. But we cannot forget that Paul and Silas, when they told the jailer what he must do to be saved, gave him instruction, without delay, respecting also his household, "Believe on the Lord Jesus Christ, and thou shalt be saved, and thy house; and they spake unto him the word of the Lord, and to all that were in his house."* When we recollect our Saviour's manifestation of his lively interest in children, and his commanding his apostles to baptize believers, 'teaching them to observe all things whatsoever I have commanded you;' when we think of the manner in which the apostles mentions Timothy's knowing the Holy Scriptures from early childhood, and of the command to parents to bring up their children in the nurture and admonition of the Lord, how can we believe that any considerable length of time elapsed before the first Christians were taught the elementary doctrine of Christian baptism, in harmony with a tender affection for their children, and a becoming interest to their spiritual welfare?

In regard to the requiring of faith, Dr. Bushnell asks, "Does it therefore follow, because it is so continually given to adults as the fixed law of salvation—he that believeth shall be saved, and he that believeth not shall be damned—that infants dying in infancy, and too young to believe, must therefore be inevitably damned? No, it will be answered, even by our Baptist brethren themselves; for the language referred to was evidently designed only for adult persons, and is of course to be qualified so as to meet the demands of reason, when we come to the case of children. And why not also the language, 'believe and be baptized?' Say not that the child is not old

* Acts xvi: 31, 32.

enough to believe, and therefore cannot be baptized. If he is not old enough to believe, how can he better be saved? Is it a greater and higher and more difficult thing to be admitted to baptism, than to be admitted to eternal glory?"

We reply: The words in the final commission (He that believeth and is baptized shall be saved; but he that believeth not shall be condemned) were, of course, never designed for any too young to believe, and as baptism is mentioned by our Lord and his apostles as a consequence of believing, there is no mention at all of one's being baptized who does not believe. Whosoever does not become a believer, there is no occasion for his being baptized; and in such a case nothing in the commission is said of baptism. This is mentioned there only in connection with believing. It is omitted in the clause that speaks of not believing. They who, through their love of sin, neglect the gospel, are condemned. Others too young to have faith or to make, understandingly and with spiritual benefit, a profession of their devotedness to the Saviour, we would lead to him in ways adapted to the 'condition of immature and infant minds,' that they may early know, and love, and obey him. In our view, to baptize them before they appear to be believers, would be to disregard our Lord's arrangement, and deprive them of its benefit. Our unauthorized act, performed upon them in their unconscious infancy, would tend to prevent their doing what, at the proper time, they should do, as conscious and confiding disciples. If, in the mean time, they be removed from our embrace and from our parental care, we would commit them, with cheerful confidence, to Him who took up little children in his arms, laid his hands upon them and blessed them, without their being baptized, and without deeming it either requisite or suitable to extend to them the ordinance of baptism. In that spiritual world of which we all know so little, he can elevate, expand, and, in every respect, prepare the once infant mind for the enjoyment of the heavenly state. At present *we see through a glass darkly*, and do not know *how* the salvation is accomplished; but we trust in the wisdom, power, and grace of our Lord Jesus Christ. "With God all things are possible." It is not for us to ask which is "greater, and higher, and more difficult," baptism or salvation? and conclude that we are to baptize all that God can save. The proper question is, What did our Lord establish as the rule for his followers here on earth? This it is for us to ascertain and observe.

After expatiating on the Pentecostal scenes at Jerusalem, in connection with the Apostle Peter's sermon, and showing that much appearing there was transient, and that much pertaining to Christianity was introduced afterwards, Dr. Bushnell at length comes to his object. "But the particular point," he says, "for which I have drawn this sketch has been purposely left behind. Infant baptism, the relation of the seminal and undeveloped first period of human existence to Christ and his flock, that which appears only implicitly in the sermon of Peter, on the day of Pentecost—where is this, and what is to come, in the way of development, here? There was no reason, or even room among the scenes of Pentecost, for so much as thinking on this subject of infants and their church relations, and scarcely more for a considerable time afterward. It could not become a subject of attention, until the church itself began to settle into forms of order and structural organization; and how soon that came to pass we do not definitely know. It should therefore be no subject of wonder that infant baptism figures somewhat indistinctly, for so long a time at least; and scarcely more, that it shows itself only by implication and a kind of tacit development for a brief time afterwards.

"Furthermore, if it came to pass by a transference of Jewish ideas into Christian spheres, Jewish modes and conditions into the Christian order and economy,—just as Peter's Jewish language, when he said, in his pentecostal speech, 'to you and to your children,' finally came back to him in its Christian power—it would make no bold and staring figure anywhere. If the Christian teachers looked to see all the better mercies of the old economy transferred into the Christian, and exalted there into some higher and more perfect meaning, we ought certainly not to expect any debate, or any thing but a silent, scarcely conscious flow of transition, when infants are taken to be with their parents, in the church, the covenant, the Christian Israel of their faith. And in just this way the defect of any bold declaration on the subject of infant baptism in the writings of the New Testament, and the fact that it appears only in a few historic glimpses, and occasional modes of speech that are subtle implications of the fact, is sufficiently accounted for."

Dr. Bushnell intimates that infant baptism came to pass, just as Peter's Jewish language, when he said, in his Pentecostal speech, 'to you and to your children,' finally came back to him in its Christian power." But what is here assumed as an illustrating fact, our readers will perceive, is only an imagination.

Had infant baptism been transferred into the Christian dispensation by a transference of Jewish ideas into Christian spheres, Jewish modes and conditions into the Christian order and economy—that is, had it, as Dr. Bushnell elsewhere represents, been intuitively transferred—it could not have failed of being mentioned somewhere in the New Testament, which so frequently and in so great a variety of connections introduces the subject of baptism. For one moment, let us think of the consultation at Jerusalem respecting circumcision, as it is recorded in the fifteenth chapter of the Acts. Here, if infant baptism came into use, either in the place of infant circumcision, or on the same principle, either among the Jewish Christians at Jerusalem, or among the Gentile Christians at Antioch, the fact could not have been passed over in silence. Let us think, too, of the account respecting Philip's preaching to the people in the city of Samaria. "When they believed Philip preaching the things concerning the kingdom of God and the name of Jesus Christ, they were baptized, both men and women." * If children were baptized on account of the faith of their parents, why does not the record add the words, *and their children?* But we will not detain our readers with instances of silence, where silence cannot be well accounted for, if there was such a practice as that of which we are speaking.

In the close of the last extract, Dr. Bushnell acknowledges that, in the New Testament, infant baptism "appears only in a few historic glimpses, and occasional modes of speech that are subtle implications of the fact." Whether it appears there at all or not, we shall by and by endeavor to ascertain, and to put our readers in the way of ascertaining.

"But," continues Dr. Bushnell, "we are inquiring after the mode in which this rite became an accepted element of the Christian organization, and a part of the church practice, as we certainly know that it did at some time afterward. Peter probably conceived as little what his language might infer respecting it, as he certainly did what hidden import there was in his testimony, by the same words, of grace to the Gentiles; for he spoke in prophetic exaltation, as the ancient prophets did, not knowing what the Spirit of Christ did signify. But suppose one of these adult

* Acts viii: 12.

converts at the Pentecost to have set off, after the few happy weeks of his sojourn are ended, for his home in some remote region of Arabia, Parthia or Greece. He carries Christ with him, he is a new man, filled with a strange joy, burning with a strange, all-sacrificing love to the cause of his new Master, and to every sinner of mankind. He begins to preach the Christ he loves to his friends, tells them all he knows of the new gospel, speaks to them as one whom Christ has endowed with the power to speak. He gathers a little circle, which we may call a church, around him, perhaps converts a little obscure synagogue into a church. He knows that he himself was baptized as a token of his faith, and he has heard a thousand times repeated, Christ's words, 'he that believeth and is baptized,' 'except a man be born of water and of the spirit,' and he does not scruple to baptize all his new fellow-disciples. Then comes the question, what of the families? what of the infants we have, who are not old enough to believe? This, on the supposition that he had heard nothing of infant baptism before he left Jerusalem, which may or may not be true. But he has heard the whole story of Christ's life many times over, including the fact of his beautiful interest in children, and his declaration, 'Of such is the kingdom.' He recollects also the ancient religion of his people; how it identified always the children with the fathers, and included them in the covenant of the fathers, raising doubtless the question, whether the gospel in its nobler, wider generosity and completer grace, would fall short even of the old religion in its tenderness to the family affections, and its provisions for the religious unity of families. And just here, we will suppose, the words of Peter, in that first sermon, flash on his recollection—'for the promise is to you and to your children.' They meant almost nothing, it may be, when they were spoken, but how full and clear the meaning they now take! It is like a revelation. The doubt struggling in his bosom is over, the question is settled. 'My children,' he says, 'are with me, one with me in my faith, included with me in all my titles and hopes, and as I came in, out of the defilements of sin, and was baptized in token of my cleansing, so too are they to share my baptism and be heirs together with me in the grace of life.'

"Thus instructed, he will baptize his children, and make his religion a strictly family grace, expecting them to grow up in it; others also consenting with him in the same conclusion, and offering their children to God in the same manner. And, as the result, they will no more be Christians with families, but Christian families—all together in the church of God. In this manner, the Pentecost itself, when the seeds that are in it are developed, will almost certainly issue the adult baptism there begun, the baptism of the three thousand, in the common baptism of the house."

As a work of imagination, the picture here presented is admirable. Why should we undertake to refute it? A voice of heavenly wisdom has proclaimed, "The prophet that hath a dream, let him tell a dream, and he that hath my word, let him speak my word faithfully. What is the chaff to the wheat? saith the Lord."*

*Jer. xxiii: 28.

IV.

THE RECEPTION OF YOUNG CHILDREN BY OUR LORD, AND APOSTOLIC AUTHORITY.

DR. BUSHNELL states (p. 152) that "Christ comes very near to a specific and formal command of infant baptsim, when we put together, side by side, what he says of baptism in the third chapter of John, and what he says concerning infants elsewhere." . . . What he said to Nicodemus, in the third chapter of John, we have already considered. Let us now see what he did and what he said concerning infants and young children, when they were brought to him, as related by the Evangelists.* "Suffer the little children," he said, "to come unto me, and forbid them not, for of such is the kingdom of God. . . . And he took them up in his arms, put his hands upon them and blessed them." He manifested the tenderest affection and regard for them, in ways adapted to their state; and thus he encouraged all to expect from him the spiritual blessings that may be needed for our children, as well as for ourselves. But he neither baptized the little ones, nor commanded them to be baptized. Had infant baptism been in accordance with his will, surely he would have

* See Matt. xix: 13, 15: Mark x: 13-16: Luke xviii: 15-17.

given some intimation of it, on an occasion so favorable.

One of the discourses in the volume before us is entitled "Apostolic Authority of Infant Baptism;" and it is based on 1 Cor. i: 16, *I baptized also the household of Stephanas.* In this Dr. Bushnell presents afresh the organic unity of the family as a ground for the baptism of infants. "The father and mother are not merely a man and a woman, but they are a man and a woman having children; and accordingly it is the father and mother, that is, the man and woman *and* their children, that are to be baptized." He adds: "It is precisely this great fact of an organic unity that is taken hold of and consecrated, in the field of religion, by the Abrahamic and other family covenants. And the whole course of revelation, both in the Old and New Testament, is tinged by associations, and sprinkled over with expressions that recognize the religious unity of families, and the inclusion of the children with the parents. All the promises run —'to you and to your children;' for Peter's language here is only an inspired transfer and re-assertion of the Jewish family ideas, at the earliest moment, in the field of Christianity itself. . . . In this universal religion, therefore, we are to look for the continuance onward of the old family character and the inclusive oneness of fathers with their children. The only difference will be that the oneness will be raised into a more spiritual and higher sense, just as every thing else was raised. The children are thus looked upon to be presumptively as believing in the faith and regenerated in the regeneration of the fathers."

Rather we would say, the children are looked upon to be what they are, children of believers, to be brought up in the nurture and admonition of the Lord;—and when they give evidence of *being* believers, they are *looked upon* to be such. Believing, like repenting, is a personal act. It cannot be performed by proxy. And the Scriptures nowhere authorize us to assume that children have faith merely because their parents have, or to account them as "regenerated in the regeneration of the fathers." On the contrary, a great principle is announced in the admonition, "Think not to say within yourselves, We have Abraham to our father."*

Dr. Bushnell proceeds: "And here again circumcision comes to our aid, as another and distinct evidence. For it was given to be 'a seal of the righteousness of faith,' and the application of it, as a seal, to infant children, involves all the precise difficulties—neither more nor less—that are raised by the deniers of infant baptism. Let the point here made be accurately understood. The argument is not that infant baptism was directly substituted for circumcision. Of this there is no probable evidence. Such a substitution could not have been made without remark, discussion, opposition of prejudice, and the raising of contentions that would have required dis-

* Matt. iii: 8

tinct mention, many times over, in the apostolic history. But the argument is this: that the Jewish mind was so familiarized by custom with the notion of an inclusive religious unity in families (partly by the rite of circumcision), that Christian baptism, being the seal of faith, was naturally and by a kind of associational instinct, applied over to families in the same manner. Not to have made such an application would have required some authoritative interposition, some dike of positive hindrance, to turn aside the current of Jewish prepossessions. And if there had risen up, somewhere, a man of Baptist notions, to ask, Where is the propriety of applying baptism, given as a rite for believers, to infants, who we certainly know are not old enough to believe? he could not even have begun to make an impression by it. Was not circumcision given to Abraham to be the seal of faith? And has it not been applied from his time down to the present, in this way—applied to infant children eight days old? True it is the doctrine of Christ, 'he that believeth and is baptized shall be saved,' and our apostles too are saying, 'If thou believest with all thy heart thou mayest.' So we all say and think, as relating to adult persons; but do we not all know that what is given to the father includes the children, and that his faith is the faith of the house? Nothing, in short, is plainer than that every argument raised to convict infant baptism of absurdity, holds, in the same manner, as convicting circumcision of absurdity, and all the religious polity of the former ages. Every such argument, too, mocks the religious feeling and conviction of all these former ages, in a way of disrespect equally presumptuous."

We reply: Abraham, as it is stated in Rom. iv: 11, "received the sign of circumcision, a seal of the righteousness of the faith which he had, yet being uncircumcised, that he might be the father of all them that believe." From him a nation was to descend who should possess the land of Canaan, and be highly favored of God. As a memorial of Abraham's acceptable faith and of the promise given, he and all his male servants, and his and their male children eight days old, were to be circumcised. This was a positive institution, having its own national object and its peculiar purport. Baptism is a positive institution, having another object and a different purport. The circumcision of infants, as well as of adults, was enjoined. The baptism of infants has not been enjoined by any competent authority. It is inconsistent with the design of baptism as represented in the Holy Scriptures. And, so far as it is practiced, it displaces and annuls what our Lord, in his wisdom, has enjoined. These are difficulties pertaining to infant baptism, which do not pertain to infant circumcision.

The argument, our author remarks, "is not that baptism was directly substituted for circumcision . . . But the argument is this: that the Jewish mind was so familiarized by custom with the notion of an inclusive religious unity in families (partly by the rite of circumcision), that Christian baptism, being the seal of faith, was naturally and by a kind of associational instinct, applied over to families in the same manner." In other words: that infant baptism came, not in the place of infant circumcision, but on the same principle of an inclusive religious unity in families; and hence that it was intuitively applied. When he speaks of Christian baptism as "being the seal of faith," he must mean the parent's faith. Baptism is never, in the Bible, called a seal. It is so called in the Shepherd or Pastor of Hermas, a religious and imaginative work of the second century, that was widely circulated, and had great influence. And the phrase seal of faith, used subsequently by ecclesiastical writers, came to be confounded with the phrase, *seal of the righteousness of faith*, used by the apostle when he speaks of the sign of circumcision given to Abraham, as a seal of the righteousness of the faith which he had, being yet uncircumcised. The first phrase had reference at first to the faith of him who received baptism, not to the faith of his parent; the second, to the justifying or acceptable character of Abraham's faith. Abraham believed God, and it was accounted to him for righteousness. Know ye, therefore, that they who are of faith, the same are the children of Abraham."* It is they who themselves believe; not they who are merely the natural offspring of a believer.

It is asked (p. 148), "Do we not all know that

* Gal. iii: 6, 7.

what is given to the father includes the children?" that is, what is given to the father is given to his children; "and that his faith is the faith of the house?" We cannot answer in the affirmative, without limitation. The pastorate of a church, or membership in a scientific society, or in some association of artists, or of mechanics, or of merchants, may be given to a father, while it is not given to his children. If his faith is to be accounted the faith of the house, so that they are to be baptized in virtue of it, why did not the apostle Paul think of this great principle when he wrote to the Corinthians, "If any brother hath a wife that believeth not, and she be pleased to dwell with him, let him not put her away."* Why did he not add, But let her without delay be baptized? for, though unbelieving, she is sanctified by her husband; she is kindly disposed towards him; and "do we not all know that his faith is the faith of the house?"

We are not conscious of deserving the charge of presumptuousness. We have already shown that for observing infant circumcision the Jews had reasons which we have not for observing infant baptism. We would let every religious institute rest on its own basis. We ask only for evidence of its having been established by competent authority. The apostles themselves were sometimes thought to act presumptuously in their efforts "to turn aside the current of Jewish prepossessions." No better apology is needed

* 1 Cor. vii: 12.

now, than that which they gave: "We ought to obey God rather than men."*

From the words of the apostle Paul in 1 Cor. vii: 14, "Else were your children unclean; but now are they holy," Dr. Bushnell draws another argument for infant baptism. But the best Biblical scholars of the present age have clearly shown that the reasoning of the apostle, in this very passage, proves the non-existence of infant baptism in his time.

Some Jewish converts, it seems, questioned the propriety of a believer's continuing to live with an unbelieving wife or husband, supposing that such intimate intercourse would be defiling. The apostle Peter once had occasion to say: "Ye know how that it is an unlawful thing for a man that is a Jew to keep company or come unto one that is of another nation," or not a member of the same religious community; "but God has showed me that I should not call any man common or unclean."† With the same enlarged Christian view the apostle Paul decides the case presented in the passage before us: Let not the believing consort thrust away the yet unbelieving. For the unbelieving husband is sanctified, so that he is not to be regarded as unclean by the wife; and the unbelieving wife is sanctified, so that she is not to be regarded as unclean by the husband. . . . He proceeds still farther to illustrate the propriety of the course that he enjoins. Addressing the Corinthian

* Acts v: 29. † Acts x: 28.

church, he says, *Else*, that is, if the representation which I have given be not correct, if the yet unbelieving, and, of course unbaptized, wife or husband must be regarded as unclean, and therefore must be abandoned, then, by a parity of reasoning, *your own children are unclean*, and must be abandoned. The little ones, because they are not yet believers, must not even touch their own Christian parents! Your very infants must not be pressed to the bosoms of their own Christian mothers! *But now* such absurdity is obvious; *but now* it is manifest that, instead of being unclean, *they are holy*, or *clean:* they are objects suitable to be administered to and cherished in all the endearing intercourse of domestic life, according to the arrangements of God for the temporal and spiritual welfare of families.

The kindred expression, *is sanctified*, used in connection with the unbelieving consort, attributes as much holiness, and holiness of the same kind, to that consort, as are attributed to the children of the Corinthian Christians. The holiness, in both cases, is freedom from such a state as would render family intercourse improper. As it did not imply the baptism of the consort not yet having faith in Christ, so it did not imply the baptism of the children not yet having faith in Christ. On the contrary, the reasoning of the apostle, all must perceive, proceeds on the assumption that *the children referred to were not yet numbered among the believers, as all persons were who had been baptized.*

So much for 1 Cor. vii: 14. We ask our readers to ponder the passage carefully, and see for themselves what it shows. Rightly understood, we are confident, it will be found by them, as it has been by others, not only to give no evidence that infants were baptized, but, on the contrary, to testify positively that they were not baptized in the time of the apostles.

And this testimony is confirmed by Gal. iii: 26, 27. There the apostle Paul says to the Galatians: "Ye are all the children of God *by faith* in Christ Jesus; for as many of you as have been baptized into Christ have put on Christ." Observe how he connects the being children of God *by faith* with being *baptized into Christ*. The believers mentioned in the 26th verse are the same persons that are mentioned in the 27th. And these are *as many as have been baptized*. These, as believers, have put on Christ. Manifestly, then, the children too young to do this had not been baptized.

In connection with the misinterpretation of 1 Cor. vii: 14, we have, on the 155th page, an instructive exhibition of the tendency of one error to produce another. It is there said, "So strong, even, is the conviction, in these apostolic times, of an organic unity sovereign over the faith and the religious affinities of children, that, where but one parent only believes, that faith carries presumptively the faith of the children with it. And upon this grand fact of the religious economy, baptism was from the first, and properly, applied to the children of them that believe. Hence, too, it was that the children of believers were familiarly addressed by them as believers; as in the epistles of Paul to the Ephesians and Colossians. The epistles are formally inscribed to churches or Christian brotherhoods: 'To the saints which are at Ephesus, and to the faithful in Christ Jesus'; 'To the saints and faithful brethren in Christ which are at Colosse.' And yet in both the children are particularly addressed: 'Children obey your parents in the Lord, for this is right;' 'Children obey your parents in all things, for this is well pleasing unto the Lord.' In this manner children are formally included among the 'faithful in Christ Jesus.'"

We rejoice that there were believing children in those churches, and that they with others who might listen to Christian instruction were encouraged to obey their parents, and thus set a worthy example for all children. We rejoice to see children now loving and honoring the Saviour as his disciples. Let them come early, and learn of Him who is meek and lowly in heart; and let them have the comfort and the benefit of expressing, in the way that he has appointed for his disciples, their childlike trust and devotedness, and of remembering the cordial consecration all their days. No one needs to be informed that the children addressed by the apostle were not mere infants.

The charge of inconsistency, which Dr. Bushnell urges against those who reject infant baptism, is remarkable: "The objectors themselves are admitting and practicing, without difficulty, observances that have comparatively no specific authority at all. At the sacrament of the Supper they use leavened bread without scruple, when they know that it was not used by Christ himself, and was solemnly forbidden at the festival he was there, in fact, re-appointing for the Christian uses of his disciples in all future ages. Where, then, is the authority given for a change even in the element of the Holy Supper itself? The Christian Lord's Day, too, accepted in the place of the Jewish Sabbath, and that even against a specific command of the Decalogue—how readily, and with how little scruple do they accept the Lord's Day and let the ancient Sabbath go, when it is only by the faintest, most equivocal, or evanescent indications that they can make out a shadow of authority for the change? 'Direct proof! positive command! specific injunction!' they say; 'without these, infant baptism has no right.' Where, then, do they get their authority for these other observances—one of them never referred to in the Scripture at all, and the others so doubtfully that infant baptism has, in comparison, the clear evidence of day?"

What is not referred to in the Scripture at all, we may safely conclude, can make no part of the institution of the Lord's Supper; and we shall be ready to practice infant baptism, when we find as much evidence for it as we have for the observance of the Lord's Day.

Still another argument is brought forward by Dr.

Bushnell, with much confidence. We present it in his own words, p. 153: "What is said in the New Testament of household baptism, or the baptizing of households, is positive proof that infants were baptized in the times of the apostles—baptized, that is, in and because of the supposed faith of the parents. The fact of such baptism is three times distinctly mentioned; in the case of 'the household of Stephanas,' of Lydia 'and her household,' and the jailor 'and all his.' In the first case, nothing is said of faith at all, though doubtless he was baptized as a believer. In the second, every thing turns on the personal faith of Lydia—'if ye have judged *me* to be faithful.' In the third, it seems to be said, according to an English translation, that all the house believed—'*he* rejoiced, believing in God, with all his house.' But the participle believing is singular and not plural in the original, and the phrase—'with all his house'—plainly belongs to the verb and not to the participle. Rigidly translated, the passage would read—'he rejoiced with all his house, himself believing.'"

The argument is easily answered. In the first case, that of Stephanas, in 1 Cor. i: 16, "I baptized also the household of Stephanas," we need only compare this with what is said near the close of the epistle, xvi: 15: "Ye know the house of Stephanas, that it is the first fruits of Achaia, and that they have addicted themselves to the ministry of the saints." Here the household is described as converts, who exerted themselves to supply the wants of their poor and afflicted fellow-disciples.

In the second case, that of Lydia, in Acts xvi: 15, "When she was baptized, and her household, she besought us, saying, If ye have judged me to be faithful to the Lord, come into my house and abide there' —we have only to read on to the end of the chapter, where it is stated, respecting Paul and Silas, when about to leave the city, after being released from prison, that they "entered into the house of Lydia; and when they had seen the brethren, they comforted them and departed." With Lydia, doubtless, were her household. She, a seller of purple, it seems, had a mercantile establishment at Philippi. Of course, she would need persons to assist her; and who can doubt that her household who had been baptized were, in part at least, the brethren who were seen and comforted?

In the third case, that of the jailor, in Acts xvi: 33, "He was baptized, he and all his, straightway," we have only to read the preceding verse,"They spake unto him the word of the Lord, and *to all that were in his house.*" "All his," who, as stated in the thirty-third verse, were baptized, are manifestly the same as "all that were in his house," to whom, as stated in the thirty-second, the word of the Lord was spoken. Besides, in the thirty-fourth verse, we are informed that he rejoiced, with all his house, having believed in God. He, with all his, or all that were in his house, having believed the word of the Lord spoken to them, rejoiced. They all rejoiced, having believed. What is said of the jailor is here said also of his household. This is clearly indicated by the phrase *with all his house.* If the word of the Lord was spoken to all that were in his house, and if he rejoiced *with all his house*—that is, he and they rejoiced together (and this is the obvious and undeniable meaning), surely we must admit that not only he but they also could and did believe. The rejoicing was a consequence of believing; and how could they participate in the joy of believing, if they had not believed? The effort to make it supposed that *they* did not believe, by inserting the word *himself* before the word believing—"himself believing"—is a very grave error. We are sorry to see it; especially in so excellent a man as Dr. Bushnell. The correctness of our interpretation is further confirmed by the case of Crispus, mentioned in Acts xviii: 8. "And Crispus, the chief ruler of the synagogue, believed on the Lord with all his house; and many of the Corinthians hearing, believed and were baptized."

In view of what has been stated respecting these and other passages, we hope that our readers will feel the duty of searching the Scriptures, and of letting the light of one portion shine upon another, till the whole subject is illuminated. This they can easily do. The Bible is at hand; and, in many cases, it is furnished with references, to facilitate comparison or examination. generally. Besides, there is an excellent little work prepared with special reference to the examination which we are now proposing. It is entitled "*The Scripture Guide to Baptism*; or a faithful Citation of all the passages of the New Testament which relate to this Ordinance; with the sacred Text, impartially examined, and the sense supported by numerous Extracts from the most eminent and learned Writers. To which is added a short examination of the Rise and Grounds of Infant Baptism. By R. Pengilly." It is written with care and with candor. It breathes the spirit of Christian love and fidelity. And the author in his final address to the candid and pious inquirer, says: "Do not allow the observations contained in this pamphlet to influence you in the smallest degree, on a subject of so sacred a nature. I would advise you to peruse the passages of Scripture again, omitting all the rest; and then form your sentiments, and govern your practice, by the pure unerring word, and that alone."

There is also another help which ought to be mentioned in this connection. It is the Rev. Dr. Hackett's Brief Statement of the best established Results at which Biblical Interpreters have arrived respecting Infant Baptism. It may be found in a small volume entitled *Baptismal Tracts for the Times.** He introduces the statement by saying, "No decision in biblical criticism, not absolutely unanimous, can be considered as better established at the present time,

* See also his Commentary on the Acts of the Apostles (xvi: 15), second edition, pp. 259–261.

than that of the utter insufficiency of these passages to prove or to justify the practice referred to, as an apostolic institution. The following testimonies of men who are admitted to possess the highest authority in regard to inquiries of this nature, may be taken as representing the attitude in which this subject now stands, as viewed in the light which the present state of biblical learning has shed upon it. It gives weight to these testimonies, that they proceed from men whose ecclesiastical position would naturally dispose them to adopt a different view; who belong to a church that practices infant baptism, and who, for the most part, contend that it is proper to adhere to it, notwithstanding their acknowledgment that the usage has no scriptural warrant."

After presenting the remarks of Meyer, Olshausen, De Wette, Neander and Rückert, Professor Hackett closes thus: "Numerous other names, hardly less distinguished, not only in this particular department of learning, but in other kindred branches, offer themselves as witnesses to the same effect. The object does not require us to extend the enumeration. The extracts presented above may be taken as exhibiting the prevalent view of the ablest authorities, at the present time, in regard to the question here discussed. We are authorized to say, that the opinion that Infant Baptism has any legitimate sanction from any passage in the New Testament is no longer a tenable opinion at the bar of Biblical criticism."

V.

EARLY CHURCH HISTORY.

BUT Dr. Bushnell has recourse to another tribunal, and proceeds thus: "Lastly, it remains to glance at the evidences from church history, or the history of the times subsequent to the age of the apostles. It has been the mood of Christian learning, in the generation past—for the learned men have moods and phases, not to say fashions, like others in the less thoughtful conditions—to make large concessions in the matter of baptism, both as regards the manner and the subjects. But a reaction is now begun, and it is my fixed conviction that it will not stop, till the encouragement heretofore given to the Baptist opinions is quite taken away. It has never been questioned, however, that infant baptism became the current practice of the church at a very early date. It is mentioned, incidentally and otherwise, in the writings of the earliest church fathers after the age of the apostles. Thus it is testified by Justin Martyr, who was probably born before the death of the apostle John: 'There are many of us, of both sexes, some sixty and some seventy years old, who were made disciples from their childhood'; and the word *made disciples* is the same that Christ himself used, when he said, 'Go, *teach* [i.e. disciple] all nations, baptizing,' etc.; the same that was currently applied to baptized children afterwards."

The representation here that the phrase *were made disciples* signifies *were baptized*, is an error, which Mr. Wall and his followers have labored strenuously to maintain, but which is sufficiently refuted by John iv: 1, where the Pharisees are mentioned as having heard 'that Jesus made *and* baptized more disciples than John.' The making of disciples is there presented as one thing; and the baptizing of them as another. The true interpretation is put beyond all question, also, by a treatise on baptism, found among the works of the celebrated Greek ecclesiastical Father, Basil the Great. The treatise consists of two books or parts. At the head of the first chapter of the first book, the author places the proposition, *That it is requisite, first to become a disciple of the Lord, and then to be accounted worthy of the holy baptism* * He quotes the command given to the apostles and remarks, "The Lord commanded first, Disciple all the nations, and then added, Baptizing them, and so forth. . . . We have thought it necessary," he says, "to recur to the order prescribed by the Lord, that thus also, knowing first the import of the command to disciple, then subsequently receiving the reason of the superlatively glorious baptism, ye may be well conducted to the completion, being

* Ὅτι δεῖ πρῶτον μαθητευθῆναι τῷ κυρίῳ, καὶ τότε καταξιωθῆναι τοῦ ἁγίου βαπτίσματος.

taught to observe all things whatsoever the Lord commanded his own disciples."*

Other Greek ecclesiastical writers explain and use the expression in the same sense, that is, as having reference to those who are capable of receiving instruction. Why, in a case like this, should we doubt their ability to understand their own language?

And then, as to the expression, 'from their childhood,' or *from children*—ἐκ παίδων—we have only to remember that the Greek word, as well as the English word, is in itself, very indefinite, and is spoken of all ages from infancy up to full-grown youth. Who does not know that it is to be explained according to the connection in which it is used? And here it is used in connection with a word which Greek writers themselves explain as indicating ability to hear, believe, and obey. Besides, in Luke viii : 5, and 54, it is used with reference to the daughter who is mentioned in the 42nd verse as being about twelve years of age; and in Acts xx : 12, it is used with reference to him who in the 9th verse is called a young man.

Justin Martyr, in his Apology for the Christians, proposes to give to the Roman Emperor an account of Christian baptism: "In what manner we dedicate ourselves to God, being new-made by Christ, we will explain, lest omitting this, we should seem to be guilty of disingenuousness in the narration." Then

---

* Vol. II., p. 624 Ben. ed.

he proceeds to present such a description as indicates clearly that the persons baptized acted deliberately and voluntarily. "As many," he says, "as are persuaded and believe that our doctrines are true, and promise to be able to live accordingly, are taught to pray, and, fasting, to ask from God forgiveness of their past sins, we praying and fasting with them. Then they are led by us to a place where there is water."* Such were the recipients of baptism; according to him, it is limited to believers—"as many as are persuaded and believe." His character and his circumstances alike forbid the supposition that he gives only a partial and deceptive account of so important a matter as initiation into the new religion, and withholds an account which he could have given respecting the initiation of infants. His silence, therefore, on this occasion especially—to say nothing of his silence elsewhere, throughout his works—shows that there was then no infant baptism to be described. Let it now be recollected that his Apology for the Christians, in which his particular account of baptism occurs, was written and presented to the

* First Apology or Defence, c. 61, p. 79, among Justini et Martyris Opera quae extant omnia, Paris ed., A.D. 1742. Ὃν τρόπον δὲ καὶ ἀνεθήκαμεν ἑαυτοὺς τῷ Θεῷ, καινοποιηθέντες διὰ ταῦ Χμισταῦ, ἐξηγησόμεθα· ὅπως μὴ τοῦτο παραλιπόντες δόξωμεν πονηρεύειν τι ἐν τῇ ἐξηγήσει. Ὅσοι ἂν πεισθῶσι καὶ πιστεύωσι ἀληθῆ ταῦτα τὰ ὑφ᾽ ἡμῶν διδασκόμενα καὶ λεγόμενα εἶναι, καὶ βιοῦν οὕτως δύνασθαι ὑπισχνῶνται, εὔχεσθαί τε καὶ αἰτεῖν νηστεύοντες παρὰ τοῦ Θεοῦ τῶν προημαρτημένων ἄφεσιν διδάσκονται, ἡμῶν συνευχομένων καὶ συννηστευόντων αὐτοῖς. ἔπειτα ἄγονται ὑφ᾽ ἡμῶν ἔνθα ὕδωρ ἐστί.

emperor Antoninus Pius, about the year 140, or near the middle of the second century.

In view of the facts to which we have adverted, our readers will not be surprised to find that the author of the recent elaborate work on the Life, Writings and Opinions of Justin Martyr, still makes the following large concessions: "Whenever Justin refers to baptism, adults appear as the objects to whom the sacred rite is administered. Of an infant baptism he knows nothing. The traces of it, which some persons believe they have detected in his writings, are groundless fancies, artificially produced. In the words, 'Many men and many women, sixty and seventy years old, who, from children, have been disciples of Christ, preserve their continence,' nothing more is said than that many individuals of both sexes became disciples of Christ in early life. The idea of being discipled—μαθητεύεσθαι—does *not* necessarily include that of being baptized; it merely brings before our mind a catechumenate. And even admitting that the baptismal rite was included in being discipled, this by no means is decisive of a reference to infant baptism. *From children*—ἐκ παίδων—contrasted with sixty and seventy years old, may well denote the entrance on the period of youth."*

Next, a passage is quoted from Irenæus, who

* Justin Martyr: His Life, Writings and Opinions; by the Rev. Charles Semisch, of Trebnitz, Silesia; translated from the German, with the author's concurrence, by J. E. Ryland. Vol. II., p. 331 and 335.

wrote in the latter part of the second century. In this, Irenæus speaks of all as being regenerated unto God; infants and little children, and lads, and young men, and older persons. Dr. Bushnell remarks: "In the phrase *regenerated unto God,* which is thus applied to infants, expressly named as distinguished from little children, he refers, it cannot be doubted, to baptism; which, being the outward sign of such inward grace, was naturally and very properly called regeneration. Infants plainly could be regenerated to God in no other sense; and therefore his language cannot even be supposed to have any meaning, if this be rejected."

Had Dr. Bushnell examined all that remains of the works of Irenæus, he would himself, we think, have been convinced that the phrase now under consideration has no reference to infant baptism. The result of such an examination, made for the purpose of ascertaining the import of this phrase, was published at Andover, in the Bibliotheca Sacra and Theological Review for November, 1849. The writer shows that, "according to Irenæus, Christ, in becoming incarnate and thus assuming his mediatorial work, brought the human family into a new relation, under himself, and placed them in a condition in which they can be saved. In this sense, he is the Saviour of all. He restored them, or summed them up anew in himself. He became, so as to speak, a second Adam, the regenerator of mankind. Through him they are regenerated unto God: *per eum renascuntur in Deum.*

The thought occurs frequently; and it is variously modified by the various connections in which it is introduced." The assumption that Irenæus is here speaking of baptism is shown to be unauthorized. "The context is against it; for the context directs our attention to *Christ* and what he himself, personally, came to do for the human family. It is by *him*, and not by baptism, that they are here said to be renewed, born anew, or regenerated. And parallel passages are against it; for they abundantly confirm the sense already given, as being the true sense of the passage before us."

For the overwhelming evidence adduced we refer our readers to the article itself.*

In regard to Tertullian, at Carthage in Africa, towards the end of the second century and in the early part of the third, Dr. Bushnell represents that his opposition to infant baptism supposes the current practice of such baptism at the time. But, manifestly, it supposes only that, in his circle, what he opposed had begun to be practiced. Nothing more than this is proved, unless in his opposition, he uses some expressions that imply the currency of the practice. Does any such evidence appear? Not at all. He is showing that baptism is not to be given rashly. "*Give to every one that asketh thee*," he adds, "has its proper subject, and relates to almsgiving; but

* It has more recently been published as one among the Baptismal Tracts for the Times, and is entitled, The Meaning of Irenæus in the phrase, *Regenerated unto God.*

that command rather is here to be considered, 'Give not that which is holy to dogs, neither cast your pearls before swine;' and that, 'Lay hands suddenly on no man, neither be partaker of other men's faults.' . . . Therefore, according to the condition and disposition and age of each person, the delaying of baptism is more beneficial, especially in the case of little ones. For what need is there that sponsors be brought into danger? They, through death, may fail of fulfilling their promises, or they may be defrauded by the coming forth of a bad disposition. The Lord does indeed say, *Forbid them not to come unto me.* Therefore let them come while they are growing up; let them come while they are learning, while they are being taught whither they are coming. Let them be made Christians [be identified by baptism with the body of Christians], when they shall have been able to know Christ. Why hastens the innocent age to the remission of sins? More caution will be used in secular matters; so that to whom earthly treasure is not intrusted, heavenly may be intrusted! Let them learn to desire salvation, that you may appear to have given to him that asketh."

So far is this appeal or expostulation from supposing and proving the current or general practice of infant baptism, that Neander mentions it as "a proof that the practice had not yet come to be regarded as an apostolic institution; for otherwise he would hardly have ventured to express himself so strongly against it." "Tertullian" he adds, "evidently means that children should be led to Christ by instructing them in Christianity; but that they should not receive baptism until, after having been sufficiently instructed, they are led, from personal conviction and by their own free choice, to seek for it with sincere longing of the heart."*

Here let it be distinctly noted that Tertullian was speaking, not of infants properly so called, but of little ones (parvuli) who had sufficient maturity to be taught lessons of Christian truth and duty. This was perceived by Bunsen, so distinguished as an investigator of civil and of ecclesiastical antiquities; and, in the work entitled Hippolytus and his Age, he says, "Tertullian's opposition is to the baptism of young, growing children; he does not say a word about new-born infants; neither does Origen, when his expressions are accurately weighed."†

From Origen, in Egypt, at Alexandria, in the first half of the third century, Dr. Bushnell adduces the two passages which have usually been quoted, and which at first seem to be decisive, in favor of infant baptism. But these have come down to us, not in the original Greek, but only in a translation made by hands accustomed to take great liberties in preparing Greek works for Latin readers. Other passages, some of which are still extant in the original Greek, are decisive against infant baptism. In the space

* History of the Christian Religion and Church, Vol. I., p. 312.

† Vol. II., p. 115, (2nd Ed.)

which we can here occupy, it would be impossible to present the facts, so as to do justice to the apparently conflicting passages, and to all the persons concerned. But we are happy in being able to assure our readers that, in the Christian Review for April, 1854, they can find a somewhat extended discussion, entitled, The Testimony of Origen respecting the Baptism of Children. It closes with these words: "We have endeavored to call forth Origen himself, as it were, and let him give his own testimony. This has been uttered in his own language, the Greek, as well as in a translation, so far as it respects the principal passages and several of the others. No room is left for suspicion of fraud or spuriousness. If we have fallen into error at any point, may we be set right. If passages, which have commonly been supposed to favor infant baptism, have been satisfactorily reconciled by us with passages which decidedly exclude it, all is well. But if this has not been done, and a passage existing only in a translation, or liable to some suspicion of spuriousness, is at variance with a passage existing still in the original Greek, or liable to no such suspicion, it is clear that preference must be given to the authority of the passage still existing in the original, or liable to no suspicion. The conclusion is easy and inevitable :—*Origen should never be quotcd in support of infant baptism.* He testifies, not only indirectly, but also directly and expressly, in regard to children as well as others, that, before being baptized, they were to be taught, and to give evidence of having duly heeded the voice of Christian instruction.

"Somewhere in the first two centuries," says Dr. Bushnell, "the ancient writing called the Shepherd, or the Shepherd of Hermas, because it purports to have been written by a teacher of that name, declares the opinion that 'all infants are in honor with the Lord, and are esteemed first of all—the baptism of water is necessary to all.'"

This very remarkable passage seems to declare that all infants must be baptized. But let us examine it a little. In the first place, the word infants is here used, doubtless, not in the strictest sense, but so as to correspond to the words used where it is said that young children received the Saviour's blessing, or where he called a little child to him, and set him in the midst of his disciples, and said, Verily I say unto you, except ye be converted, and become as little children, ye shall not enter into the kingdom of heaven; whosoever, therefore, shall humble himself as this little child, the same is greatest in the kingdom of heaven,' or where the apostle Paul says,'In malice be ye children.' The phrase 'all infants,' in this connection, must mean all childlike persons; or, as Archbishop Wake has well expressed the sense of these words, "all such children." His translation of the whole paragraph, in which this phrase occurs, is as follows: "Whosoever, therefore, said he [the Shepherd] shall continue as children without malice, shall be more honorable than all those of whom I have yet spoken; for all such children are honored by the Lord, and esteemed the first of all. Happy, therefore, are ye who shall remove all malice from you, and put on innocence; because ye shall first see the Lord."

But where is the latter part of Dr. Bushnell's quotation? The nearest semblance of it that can be found is at the distance of more than ten pages, where the Shepherd is explaining what appears in the vision as stones, representing the ancient patriarchs, coming out of the deep, and being placed in the building of the tower. "It was necessary, said he, for them to ascend by water, that they might be at rest. For they could not otherwise enter into the kingdom of God, but by laying aside the mortality of their former life. They, therefore, being dead, were nevertheless sealed with the seal of the Son of God, and so entered into the kingdom of God. For before a man receives the name of the Son of God, he is ordained unto death; but when he receives that seal, he is freed from death, and assigned unto life. Now that seal is the water of baptism, into which men go down under the obligation unto death, but come up appointed unto life. Wherefore to those also was this seal preached, and they made use of it, that they might enter into the kingdom of God. And I said, why then, sir, did these forty stones also ascend with them out of the deep, having already received that seal? He answered, Because these apostles and teachers, who preached the name of the Son of God, dying after they had received his faith and power, preached to them who were dead before, and they gave this seal to them. They went down therefore into the water with them, and again came up. But these went down whilst they were alive, and came up again alive; whereas those who were before dead, went down dead, but came up alive. Through these, therefore, they received life, and knew the Son of God; for which cause they came up with them, and were fit to come into the building of the tower, and were not cut, but put in entire; because they died in righteousness, and in great purity; only this seal was wanting to them. Thus you have the explanation of these things."

The author of the writing here quoted, misapprehending the words of our Lord in the third chapter of John, has such an impression of the necessity and efficacy of baptism that he dreams of the ancient patriarchs being baptized in the state of the dead! The apostles must go to the invisible abode of the departed, and preach to them, and give them the seal of the Son of God, the water of baptism? His work, as we have already had occasion to remark, was written, probably, about the middle of the second century. It breathes a lovely spirit of Christian kindness, zeal, humility, and conscientiousness. It has a charm somewhat like that of the Pilgrim's Progress. Glowing with piety as well as with imagination, and containing many wholesome admonitions, and much important truth mingled with some pernicious error, it was widely circulated; and it could not fail of having a great influence, both for good and for evil, on the Christian community in the second, and third, and subsequent centuries. As, with all its excellencies, it seems to contain some of the seminal principles which led, at length, to the Romish doctrines of supererogation, penance, and purgatory, so it contains the seminal principles which, with other influences, led, at length, to the baptism of infants, namely, the absolute necessity and mysterious efficacy of baptism. But it contains no intimation that the baptism of infants had already begun to be practiced.

Men often adopt principles which it is easier to hold as theories, than to apply and carry out in real life; especially when institutes, either divine or human, and the usages of a numerous and widely extended community stand in the way. Often, too, men apply a principle in one direction, without applying it in others to which it is equally applicable. Time and favoring circumstances are requisite in order to diffuse and establish the principle, to awaken sufficient interest in its application, and to overcome all the obstacles. Thus the visionary and theoretical baptism of the ancient patriarchs in the state of the dead, preceded a considerable length of time the actual baptism of dying babes.

In the first part of the short sentence which is presented as a quotation from the words ascribed to Hermas, nothing is said of baptism; and in the second part nothing is said of children. If Dr. Bushnell wishes to use Hermas as an authority for the absolute necessity of baptism, especially in regard to the holy patriarchs, after they had departed from this world, we do not think it needful to detain our readers by making any particular objection.

We pass to the evidence for infant baptism which he derives from inscriptions on the monuments of children, "considered," he remarks, "by antiquarians to be of a very early age, probably of the first two or three centuries, in which they are called *fideles*, that is, *faithfuls*, just as children are addressed by Paul among the 'faithful brethren' of Ephesus and Colosse. The following is an example—(Buonarotti, 17; Fabretti, cap. 4,) 'a faithful among faithfuls, here lies Zosimus. He lived two years one month and twenty-five days.'"

Sometimes a bright and lovely child, no older than this, has begun to think and to speak, to ask questions and to make replies, in a manner that has touched the heart of a pious parent. The dear little one says that he loves the Lord Jesus Christ that died for him, and he can repeat the creed, and make the responses required for the candidate for baptism. The child mentioned in the inscription, if all that is claimed in this case be reliable, had, indeed, a maturity that is rare and admirable in one so young. His being numbered so early among the faithful, that is, the believing, was remarkable. It somewhat exceeded even the earliest limit mentioned in a celebrated sermon by Gregory Nazianzen, when bishop of Constantinople, near the close of the fourth century.

After urging on the people the importance of being baptized, he adds: "But what, it may be asked, would you say concerning those who are yet infants, not comprehending either the detriment or the benefit? Shall we baptize these also? By all means, if any danger be imminent; for it is better that they be sanctified without their knowing it, than that they die without being sealed and initiated. . . . But concerning the others I recommend that—waiting three years, either a little less or a little more, when they are able to hear and answer somewhat that pertains to the ordinance, though not understanding perfectly, yet receiving impressions—you thus sanctify both their souls and their bodies by the great mystery of initiation."*

The age of little Zosimus was a few days less than two years and two months. Instead of being almost three, he was only a little more than two years old. This made his case specially interesting. It constituted a memorable distinction; and as a distinction, as something extraordinary, it might be inscribed on his monument. Moreover had all children of believers, as a matter of course, been baptized, there would

* Τί δ' ἂν εἴποις περὶ τῶν ἔτι νηπίων, καὶ μήτε τῆς ζημίας ἐπαισθανομένων, μήτε τῆς χάριτος· ἢ καὶ ταῦτα βαπτίσομεν; πάνυ γε, εἴπερ τις ἐπείγῃ κίνδυνος. κρεῖσον γὰρ ἀναισθήτως ἁγιασθῆναι ἢ απελθεῖν ἀσφράγιστα καὶ ἀτέλεστα . . . περὶ δὲ τῶν ἄλλων δίδωμι γνώμην, τὴν τριετίαν ἀναμένοντας, ἢ μικρὸν ἐντὸς τούτου, ἢ ὑπὲρ τοῦτο, ἡνίκα καὶ ἀκοῦσαί τι μυστικὸν καὶ ἀποκρίνεσθαι δυνατόν, εἰ καὶ μὴ συνιέντα τελείως, ἀλλ' οὖν τυπούμενα, οὕτως ἁγιάζειν καὶ ψυχὰς καὶ σώματα τῷ μεγάλῳ μυστηρίῳ τῆς τελειώσεως. Orat. XL. Works of Gregory Nazianzen, Vol. I. p. 658. Paris, 1609.

have been no occasion to speak of his pre-eminence in this respect.

Thus much we might say, even if all that has been claimed for the argument from monumental inscriptions ought to be admitted. But we think that there is an impropriety in the inscription adduced by Dr. Bushnell. We allude to the improper and unjustifiable manner in which the word *believer*, or faithful (fidelis), is used; and respecting this we shall soon have occasion to speak more fully. In the next place, we cannot admit that the epitaphs to which he refers are of so early an age as to furnish a valid argument for proving infant baptism to be a part of primitive Christianity.

Natural caves and subterranean excavations, whether at Rome or elsewhere, we have reason to believe, were occasionally used by Christians in times of early persecution, as places of refuge, and where religious services might be performed, especially on days commemorating the death of martyrs. How early they were used as cemeteries it is impossible now to ascertain.

In the peaceful times under the emperor Alexander Severus (A.D. 222–235), Calixtus, the bishop of Rome, enlarged one of the subterranean vaults, and furnished it with conveniences for performing worship and religious rites. It is the cemetery of Calixtus under the magnificent church of St. Sebastian; and it first received the name *catacomb*, a name afterwards applied to other underground burying places. One of his successors, Sextus II., and four deacons, were put to death in this cemetery, in accordance with the persecuting edict of Valerian, in the year 258.*

Maximinus, in 311, forbade the Christians to enter the subterranean places of burial.† But Constantine the Great, about the year 313, restored to them their cemeteries and chapels.‡ And from his time, the burial places were prepared with increased forethought and system. They could be visited without fear or molestation; and they were honored more and more, in connection with the increasing honor paid to martyrs. Wherever the body of a martyr was deposited, his sympathizing brethren would love to repair, and strengthen their own faith by meditation and religious services. It was natural and commendable to desire for themselves, and for their kindred and friends, a quiet resting place near the graves of those dear and honored ones whose precious remains were already sleeping there. When the conveniences of the people in the vicinity, and of the multitudes attracted to the holy place, required it, a church edifice, over the place of subterranean repose, could be erected, having an easy and safe communication with the vaults beneath.

---

* See Cypriani Epist. ad Successum, etc., LXXXII. Ben. ed. p. 165—Xistum autem in cemeterio animadversum sciatis octavo iduum Augustarum die, et cum eo diacones quatuor.

† Euseb. Eccles. Hist. B. IX. ch. 2; and B. VII. ch. 11.

‡ Euseb. Life of Constantine, B. II. ch. 40.

In Rome, for several ages, till after the middle of the fifth century, the bishops were buried in the catacombs. Leo, denominated the Great, was the first exception. In the year 462 he was buried, not in a catacomb, but in the vestibule of the vestry at St. Peter's. Persons of distinction followed his example. Many were buried in the courts of the city churches, or in the sepulchres connected with them. The common people still continued to be buried in the catacombs. But the example of the superior classes had great influence. And when, for suitable honor, the bones of the martyrs themselves were removed to the city churches, the zeal for the former places of burial died away. The places were comparatively neglected. They fell into a state unfit for use; and in the seventh or eighth century they ceased entirely to be used as cemeteries, and were almost forgotten amidst the public calamities of the times.*

In 1535 some of these dark and dilapidated caverns were explored. A deep interest was awakened. Bosio, a zealous antiquary, spent more than thirty years, the last thirty years of the sixteenth century, in clearing away the rubbish, and penetrating into recesses that had been blocked up for ages. His work in Italian, on *Subterranean Rome,* was translated into Latin and enlarged by Arringhi, in two folio volumes, published at Paris in 1659. Since that time there have appeared several other interest-

* See Arringhi, Roma Subterranea, Tom. II., p. 221.

ing and, in various respects, valuable works on discoveries made in the catacombs.

Among these discoveries are inscriptions on the monuments of children. Some years ago, in a volume entitled *Apostolic Baptism*, an array of these inscriptions, gathered from Bosio, Arringhi, Muratori, Buonarotti, Fabretti, Gruter and Boldetti, was presented to the public for the purpose of proving the apostolic authority for infant baptism. We welcome any competent and credible witnesses that can be summoned. Let the dead rise from their graves. Let them be called forth from the catacombs. Their testimony may be valuable concerning the times in which they lived. But let us not be so unreasonable as to expect them to testify concerning what was done in times long before they existed, or in spheres beyond their knowledge.

The volume to which we allude presents us *thirty-two* inscriptions respecting children. *Ten* are called believers (fideles). And the age of these, except only that of Zosimus (the case adduced as an example by Dr. Bushnell), exceeds the age at which Gregory Nazianzen recommends that children be baptized, as being "able to hear and answer somewhat that pertains to the ordinance; though not understanding perfectly, yet receiving impressions." *Four* are mentioned as being "with the holy," or "with holy spirits." *One* is mentioned as being "in the bosom of Abraham, Isaac and Jacob." *One*, at the age of four years, five months, and three days, is mentioned, expressly, as a catechumen, "resting in peace." *One*, who died soon after the beginning of the fourth century, a little more than eleven years of age, is spoken of without any mention of baptism; for it is too much to assume that this is implied in his having two names, Simplicia and Colonymus. Frequently a person had more than one name, and was called sometimes by one of them, and sometimes by the other. The inscription itself, in the present case, says nothing of martyrdom, or of violence. *Fifteen* are designated as newly baptized.

Of two brothers, one who died at the age of seven years, is called a *believer* (fidelis); and the other, who died at the age of somewhat more than eight years, is said to be *newly baptized.* That is, one child, a lad of seven years, had received baptism before he was seized with his last and fatal sickness; another, in the same family, a lad of eight years and more, not having received it previously, received it now, probably in view of his danger, and thus he dies *newly baptized.* The time of his death, it is important to remember, was about the end of the fourth century, A.D. 394. What was the case with him was, doubtless, in effect, the case with most of the rest of the fifteen who are mentioned as newly baptized; and more than half of them were more than six years of age. Hence more than half of them were not baptized before arriving at that degree of maturity.

Thus, it will be perceived, when we examine and

analyze the evidence derived from these thirty-two witnesses, that instead of proving the apostolic authority of infant baptism, it harmonizes with and confirms our representations. Whatever might be the dreams of such sincere and attractive writers as Hermas, or the theories adopted by many zealous church-teachers, the practice of baptizing infants came in but gradually. Some, through the influence of erroneous views that were coming to prevail, were hastened to baptism, "though understanding imperfectly," or even not at all. More were kept waiting several years; some for an increased degree of maturity and preparation, and some for an increased probability of retaining the grace which was supposed to be received with that great remedy for all previous sin; but were baptized when danger of death was imminent, and thus died newly baptized. Some were not baptized at all; and yet, like the catechumen mentioned, were believed by their kindred and guardians to be "resting in peace," or "with the holy," through the grace of him who had said of other little ones that had not been baptized, *"Of such is the kingdom of heaven."*

Here we might confidently leave the argument from the inscriptions on the monuments of children. But we have more to say respecting the case of Zosimus; and we wish to let our readers see how the argument stands in the light of some additional discoveries.

In the recent French work, by M. Louis Perret, on

the Catacombs of Rome, we have a highly valuable contribution to the history of ancient Christian art, and of some things connected with it. The work consists of six folio volumes; five of engravings, and one of descriptions. It is exact, comprehensive, and splendid. Among other interesting objects it presents nearly *ninety* epitaphs or inscriptions respecting children. Only nine of these make any reference to baptism ; and five of this small number are included also among the thirty-two whose testimony we have already considered. Three children are mentioned as *newly baptized.* They died, one at the age of two years, five months, and twenty-five days ; one, of one year and ten months ; and one apparently of eighty days, though the inscription is very imperfect and uncertain.

Besides these two or three cases, in which it appears that a child was baptized when about to die, another is mentioned in which a child (very improperly, we think) is spoken of as a believer (fidelis) :"Florentius has made an inscription to his well-deserving son Apronianus, who lived a year, nine months, and five days. As he was much loved by his grandmother, and she saw that he was about to die, she requested of the church that he might depart from the world a believer." *

* Florentius filio suo Aproniano fecit titulum bene merenti, q (ui) vixit annum et menses nove (m), dies quinque. Cum soldu amatus fuisset a majore sua, et vidit hunc morti constitutum esse, petivit de ecclesia ut fidelis de seculo recessisset.

Here, manifestly, the church was supposed to possess a mysterious power; and the dying child was to be prepared by it, not, indeed, to grow up in the faith of his parents, as Dr. Bushnell would say, but to depart from the world a believer. Was this in accordance with the Saviour's command, and with apostolic doctrine and practice?

When were the inscriptions written? This can be ascertained in regard to those which mention the Roman consuls at the time, and hence have been called consular. In regard to the others, there is uncertainty. The earliest of all the consular inscriptions said to have been found in the catacombs is one that corresponds with our A.D. 98;* the next earliest, A.D. 107;† and then one A.D. 111.‡ These three are presented by Boldetti as having been found in one of the oldest cemeteries, that of St. Lucina, on the Ostian way, connected with the subterranean chapel which, as we have already stated, was enlarged and fitted up by Calixtus, in the first part of the third century. It seems evident, therefore, that in the second century the catacombs, to some extent, were used by Christians as places for burying their dead. But those earliest inscriptions, it must be borne in mind, say nothing respecting baptism.

* D. M.
P. Liberio vixit ani n. II. menses n. III. dies n. VIII.
R. Anicio Fausto et Virio Gallo coss.

† N. XXX. Surra et senec. coss.

‡ Servilia. Annorum XIII., Pis et Bol. coss.

The earliest allusion to the baptism of a child is A.D. 348, the child being, at the age of six years, eight months, and eleven days, newly baptized. The next earliest is A.D. 371, the child being, at the age of eight years, and fifteen days, newly baptized; and the next after this, A.D. 374, the child being, at the age of eight years, newly baptized. All these, it will be perceived, occur in the fourth century. Besides these, there are twelve consular inscriptions relative to children, without any mention of baptism; eight in the fourth century; three in the fifth; and one in the sixth.

Dr. Bushnell speaks of the inscriptions without discrimination; and he supposes them to be "of a very early age, probably of the first two or three centuries." But a careful examination proves that the very example which he has selected, namely, the epitaph of Zosimus, could have had no existence till a considerable time after the beginning of the fourth century.

This inscription is preserved in the gallery of the Vatican at Rome. It was taken from the cemetery of St. Agnes.* This holy young maiden and martyr was a victim of the persecution under the emperor Diocletian, according to Fleury, in the year 304, and according to Ruinart, in the year 306. She was condemned to be dishonored in one of those caverns of the race course that served as a brothel. For her

* See M. Perret, *Catacombes de Rome*, vol. VI., p. 154.

faith and firmness she was beheaded. Her martyrdom was the occasion of establishing there, in due time, services of devout commemoration; and there, at length, came to be the consecrated cemetery and the renowned church of St. Agnes.*

A fac-simile of the Greek original of the inscription which has occasioned these remarks, is presented by Perret in his splendid work on the Catacombs of Rome. It is one of the nearly ninety that we have mentioned. The following is a literal translation:—A believer descended from believers (πιστὸς ἐκ πιστῶν) I Zosimus lie here, having lived two years, one month, and twenty-five days.

Respecting the improper and unjustifiable manner in which the word believer is here used, we shall soon, as we have already intimated, have an opportunity of speaking more fully than we have yet done. The record before us, in whatever manner it may be explained, cannot testify for the times in which the apostles lived. It is far too late. It must now be acknowledged by all to be at least considerably later than the beginning of the fourth century; for the time and the circumstances of the martyrdom of St. Agnes preclude the possibility of supposing the

* See Fleury, Histoire Ecclésiastique, Liv. VIII., Tom. II., p. 485. Ruinart, Acta sincera, p. 504; and Description of Rome, (Beschreibung der Stadt Rom) by Platner, Bunsen Gerhood, and Röstell, vol. I., p. 401.

earlier existence of a Christian cemetery in the subterranean haunts of revelry and licentiousness near the race course.

In the same discourse, at Constantinople, from which we made a quotation, Gregory Nazianzen, speaking of various classes of persons who die without baptism, mentions one class as being those whose failure of being baptized is *on account of infancy;—from ignorance.** These, he thinks, will be neither glorified nor punished by the righteous Judge. The passage to which we now allude, and the manner in which, in the former one, he recommends the baptism of children, show that it was not uncommon in his time for children to remain unbaptized on account of infancy, which, for the most part, naturally involves a state of ignorance. He, himself, though born after his father became a bishop, and most carefully educated, it is well known, was not baptized till he arrived at a period of maturity. The deferring of his baptism, surely, could not have arisen from any desire that he might continue to sin as long as possible. And his recommending to defer the baptism of children, except when danger of death is imminent, till "they are able to hear and answer somewhat that pertains to the ordinance," surely, also, could not have arisen from any desire that they might continue to sin as long as possible. No. It must have arisen from a yet lingering impression of

* διὰ νηπιότητα.—ἐξ ἀγνοίας.

what was originally required and was according to primitive usage.

If "baptism was sometimes deferred on superstitious grounds, till severe illness; even in the hope of sinning with less danger till the performance of the rite;"—this was one of the fruits of mistaking the design of baptism, and unwarrantably ascribing to the baptismal act a mysterious efficacy; while the same prolific error, the ascribing of a mysterious, saving efficacy to the baptismal act, urged its being prematurely performed on the unprepared, and especially on the dying child. Between the unjustifiable delaying and the unjustifiable hastening of baptism there was a middle course, which, to say the least, many would gladly have followed.

Maitland, an English author, in his work entitled, *The Church in the Catacombs*, furnishes us with six epitaphs of children, not included among those which we have enumerated. One of the children died at the age of a year and nine months, newly baptized. In connection with the five others, no mention is made of baptism. One of these is expressly mentioned as a catechumen, who lived nine years, eight months, and twenty-two days. Of course it is certain that this child was not baptized, but was receiving preparatory religious instruction. He gives also an epitaph, included among those which we have already examined, that of a child who died at the age of three years and thirty days, newly baptized; and he remarks that "her extreme youth proves the custom of infant baptism."* We learn from another source that the child died A.D. 367. And he might well have said, the evidence here proves that, in the latter part of the fourth century, a child, three years old, had not been baptized, but being then about to die, there was administered to her the ceremony which was supposed by many to have, in such an extremity, the wondrous power of securing eternal salvation.

A highly respected author in our own country, the Right Rev. Dr. Kip, missionary Bishop of California, in a work entitled, "The Catacombs of Rome, as illustrating the church of the first three centuries," says, with reference to the inscriptions found there: "But there is one important truth which we think we learn from these inscriptions, and that is, the fact of infant baptism. We meet with the epitaphs of children who are called neophytes, a title which, of course, would not have been bestowed upon them unless they had been received by baptism into the church. The age at which they died precludes the idea of that rite having been administered to them in any way but as infants:

"'To Romanus, a well deserving neophyte, who lived eight years.'

"'Flavia Jovina, who lived three years and thirty days a neophyte. In peace (she died) the eleventh kalends.'

"'The title of Candidus, a neophyte, who lived twenty-one months; buried on the nones of September.'"†

* P. 281, London, 1847.

† P. 162.

The inscription for *Romanus* is a consular one—that is, one in which the names of the consuls are mentioned (Gratian and Probus), and thus the time of his death is known to have been A.D. 371. The date is entirely omitted by Bishop Kip, but it is mentioned by M. Perret and by others. The inscription for *Flavia Jovina* is the one which Maitland represents as proving Infant Baptism. The time of her death was A.D. 367; but the indication of the time is entirely omitted by him and by Bishop Kip. Both of these inscriptions, as well as the third—that of the little child *Candidus*, here adduced also for the support of infant baptism—we have already had occasion to examine in the earlier part of this discussion. It will be perceived that they can give no valid testimony. The third presents no indication of the period in which the child died. Here is no evidence whatever of this case being earlier than the two preceding cases, which occurred in the latter part of the fourth century.

Here, then, we have three children—one dying at the age of twenty-one months, or one year and nine months; another dying at the age of three years and thirty days; and still another dying at the age of eight years: all neophytes or newly baptized. They appear to have been baptized, not soon after birth, as a matter of course, but in cases of emergency just before manifestly approaching death, as a matter of necessity; it being on the one hand deemed desirable and important for children to attain to such a degree of maturity as that they could make a personal profession of faith, and on the other, in cases of special danger, to receive in some way, at all events, a passport to the bliss of heaven. For, in the latter part of the fourth century, and even earlier, the opinion had come to be very prevalent that the baptismal ceremony was absolutely necessary for salvation. But that this opinion was not yet received by all is evident from the epitaphs of catechumens, as we have already had occasion to show, and from other sources. Bishop Kip himself says, "The following epitaph is that of a catechumen; for in primitive times the training of the church began from the earliest age:

"Ucillianus to Bacius Valerius, a catechumen, who lived nine years, eight months, and twenty-two days."*

This inscription, too, has already passed under our review; and our readers will see in it an evidence that the baptism of children was not deemed by all to be necessary to every one. The distinction between the catechumens and the baptized is well known: a catechumen was one who was receiving instruction in order to be prepared for baptism.

The brief but well conceived and very attractive work of which we are here speaking, ought not to have been marred by an attempt to make these monumental inscriptions testify in favor of a practice not found in the Holy Scriptures. "The fact of infant baptism," when an infant was about to die, in the

---

* P. 160.

latter part of the fourth century, is far from being reliable evidence of what our Lord instituted or his apostles sanctioned. A book professing to illustrate the church of the first three centuries is naturally understood to present what pertains to the church in each of those centuries, and if any thing is admitted which belongs in a later century, and not in each of the earlier, the date of it manifestly ought, if possible, to be mentioned; otherwise the readers are likely to be deceived. In future editions, therefore, we hope that the author's love of Christian and historical truth will lead him to make the needed correction, to inform his readers *when* the children were baptized, or omit the argument altogether.

In regard to the case decided by the council over which Cyprian presided, at Carthage, in Northern Africa, about the middle of the third century, we need only call the attention of our readers to one consideration. We allude to what is disclosed by the nature of the case presented for decision. We say nothing here respecting the merits of the decision itself, which was, that no one, however young, was to be debarred from baptism and the grace of God, and thus be lost. The question was, whether baptism was ever to be administered before the eighth day after the birth of a child, or whether it was not rather to follow the law of circumcision, in this respect. Now, if infant baptism had been in use all along from the first, instances innumerable must have occurred in which infants, especially those in special danger of death before their eighth day, were baptized before that day. The usage, in such circumstances, must have been known; and there could have been no occasion for discussing and deciding the matter. Infant baptism, then, could not have been of long standing. It must have been just coming into existence; for it needed to be regulated as no institute properly established and well known could have needed.

But, though we regard the consideration here presented as more than a sufficient reply to all that has been, and all that can be, urged in favor of infant baptism from the decision of this council at Carthage, a little after the middle of the third century, yet it may be useful to mention a few additional facts pertaining to the subject.

1. It is here that the baptism of infants, or babes, makes its first appearance in ecclesiastical history. 2. Cyprian, in his epistle to Fidus, in the name of the council, does not place the decision on the ground of any ordinance of our Lord, or of any tradition from the apostles. 3. He does place it on the ground "that the mercy and grace of God is to be denied to none born of man. For since the Lord says in his gospel: *The Son of man is not come to destroy men's lives, but to save them*, as far as in us lies, if it can be, no soul must be lost." 4. From this epistle it is perfectly manifest that he regarded the administration

of baptism as the bestowing of salvation. 5. He believed, as is abundantly evident from other writings of his, that still in his time there were new revelations, and that what was then revealed, or could be shown to be lawful and conducive to salvation, ought to supersede what had already been practiced, "for which thing," he says, "Paul also, looking forward and faithfully consulting concord and peace, laid down the rule in his epistle, saying: *But let the prophets speak two or three; and let the others judge. But if any thing be revealed to another sitting by, let the former one be silent.* Here he taught and showed that many things are revealed to individuals for the better, and that each ought not pertinaciously to contend for what he once imbibed and held; but willingly embrace it, if any thing better or more useful be presented."*

In this passage Cyprian is defending his course in regard to the baptizing of heretics, but the principle is equally applicable to other subjects. He, and unnumbered thousands of his contemporaries, had im-

* Cui rei Paulus quoque prospiciens et concordiæ et paci fideliter consulens in epistola sua posuit dicens; Prophetæ autem duo aut tres loquantur, et caeteri examinent. Si autem alii revelatum fuerit sedenti, ille prior taceat. Qua in parte docuit et ostendit multa singulis in melius revelari et debere unumquemque non pro eo quod semel imbiberat et tenebat pertinaciter congredi, sed si quid melius et utilius extiterit libenter amplecti. Epist. to Quintus; 71. Comp. Epist. to Pompeius; 74. Ben. ed.

bibed the opinion that baptism was necessary for salvation to all, even to the unconscious infant. He claimed to have visions and revelations. Through his zeal, his glowing eloquence, his high ecclesiastical position, and his consummate skill in storms of controversy, his influence was powerful while he lived; and, when he died a martyr, it became immense. It extended itself to distant countries, and it has continued to be felt from generation to generation, down to the present time. He thought himself inspired, and thus entitled to give new directions promotive of salvation; and, doubtless, he supposed that the Holy Spirit guided the bishops, especially when assembled in full council. With these views, he could not fail of being prompted by all the compassionate feelings of his ardent mind to make the most strenuous efforts in favor of what seemed to him so important and efficacious an expedient.*

* There can be no mistake in what we have said respecting the claims of Cyprian. To his presbyters and deacons he expresses himself thus: For, which the more moved and compelled me to write this epistle unto you, ye ought to know (since the Lord has deigned to manifest and reveal it), that it was thus declared, *in a vision*, etc., Epist. xi. 3, Oxford Ed. Trans., p. 25. Know, dearest brethren, I was, not long since, reproved in a vision for this also; that we were drowsy in prayer, and watched not therein. Epist. xi. 5, p. 26. For the least of all his servants, although set in the midst of very many sins, and unworthy of his favor, did he, out of his goodness towards us, give this charge: *Bid him be secure; for peace is at hand.* Epist.

In other countries, the same opinion, that baptism is absolutely necessary to all for salvation, was more and more generally admitted; and it was producing its effects in various ways. One of the most remark-

---

xi. 7, p. 27. The Oxford translators remark that, "at the time of this vision, there was no human prospect of the cessation of the persecution; it did cease shortly after in consequence of the sudden and unexpected overthrow and death of Decius, in his expedition against the Goths." In another communication Cyprian says, The divine censure ceases not to chastise us by night and day; for, *besides nightly visions*, by day also the innocent age of children among us is filled with the Holy Ghost, and in ecstasy they see with their eyes, and hear, and speak those things wherein the Lord vouchsafed to admonish and instruct us. But ye shall hear all when the Lord, who bade me retire, shall bring me back to you. Epist. xvi. 3, p. 42. To the presbyters, deacons, and all the people, he writes: Exult, therefore, and rejoice with us, when you read our epistle, wherein I and my colleagues who were with me, report to you that Celerinus, our brother, renowned alike for his courage and his character, has been joined to our clergy, not by human suffrage, but by divine favor; who, when he hesitated to assent to the church, was, by her own admonition and exhortation *in a vision by night, compelled not to hold out against our persuasions.* Epist. xxxix. 1, p. 87. In an epistle to Florentius, he says: I remember what has been already shown to me [in visions]: yea, what has been enjoined by the authority of our Lord and God to an obedient and fearing servant. Among other things which he vouchsafed to manifest and reveal, he added this also: "Whoso therefore believeth not Christ appointing a bishop, shall hereafter begin to believe him avenging a

able of these is the impress that it has left on that singular product of the third and fourth centuries, the work claiming to be the Constitutions of the Holy Apostles. In this work we hear, as it were, an imploring voice for the infants; while Ambrose, the renowned bishop of Milan, in the fourth century, utters the prevalent conviction of his times in the following authoritative terms: "No one ascends into the kingdom of heaven but through the sacrament of baptism. . . . There is no exception even of an infant, or of a person prevented by any necessity. Such may not be openly and positively punished; but I have no assurance that they may participate in the honor of the kingdom."*

---

bishop." Although I am aware that to some persons dreams appear ridiculous and visions trifling, yet assuredly it is to such as had rather believe against bishops, than believe the bishop. Epist. lxvi. 8, p. 207, 208.

Writing to Cornelius in the name of a council, Cyprian makes the following statement: We have decided, the Holy Spirit suggesting, and the Lord, by many and plain visions, admonishing, etc. [Placuit nobis, sancto spiritu suggerente, et Domino per visiones multas et manifestas admonente.] Epist. liv. Ben. ed, p. 70, Oxford Ed. lvii. Trans. p. 141.

* De Abrah. lib. ii. c. 11. Nemo adscendit in regnum cœlorum, nisi per sacramentum baptismatis. . . Utique nullum excipit, non infantem, non aliqua præventum necessitate. Habeant tamen illam opertam pœnarum immunitatem; nescio an habeant regni honorem. The Works of Ambrose, Tom. i., pp. 347 and 351. Paris, 1686.

Still, in the most parts of Christendom, a deep impression was prevalent that faith was requisite in order to be baptized, as well as that baptism was requisite in order to be admitted into heaven. With such impressions, who that had parental affection would not have special desire, who would not earnestly pray, that the dear little ones might arrive at that state in which, as Origen expresses it, they could *be made capable of receiving the grace of Christ?* Passages occurring in some of the early Christian writers help us to understand the prayers that were offered for the infants, whether of the church or of the catechumens. These prayers, except the one which is recorded by Chrysostom as having been used by the church at Antioch, and which is in remarkable harmony with the others, are still found in the liturgical part of the Eighth Book of the Constitutions; a part which, as to its general frame-work and many of its materials, has evident marks of having been derived from ancient usage in that venerable and influential church. These prayers, though in their present form, written not earlier, probably, than the fourth century, were intended and adapted to be received as having come down from a much earlier period. They touch a tender chord in the heart of the Christian parent, and shed an unexpected light on the history of Infant Baptism. They show that *infants were not baptized.* For the burden of these prayers is, that the little ones may be brought to such an age and state as to receive baptism—this being a 'sacrament for the believers,'* without which it was generally supposed none could inherit the bliss of heaven.

In the fifteenth chapter of the Sixth Book, immediately after an admonition on the danger of sudden death, there is an ambiguous injunction for the baptism of children: "Moreover, baptize your children, and bring them up in the nurture and admonition of the Lord. For he saith, Suffer the little children to come unto me, and forbid them not."

The indefiniteness of the command seems to have been skillfully adapted to the securing of its reception as having been derived from the apostles. It could be explained so as to harmonize with the well-known apostolic practice of Believers' Baptism. For in the days of the apostles, there were, doubtless, many Christian, believing children. To have children of this character is mentioned among the qualifications of the men who were to be ordained as elders.† Children and other disciples went with Paul out of the city of Tyre, when he departed; and the company kneeled down on the shore and prayed.‡ Children that give evidence of true and intelligent faith in Christ, we all agree, ought to be baptized. The command now under consideration may have had in view such young catechumens—little disciples whom the apostles

* See Origen on Exodus, Homily viii, sect. 4, and the Christian Review for April, 1854, p. 203.

† Tit. i: 6.

‡ Acts xxi: 5.

would not have rejected; and, so understood, it could easily be regarded as apostolical. But as it places baptism prominently in the foreground, and leaves out of sight the grand prerequisite, it could also be explained so as to favor and sanction the baptism of children in early infancy. Its influence would, of course, be silent, but none the less powerful and extensive. It called for no public discussion, and no enactment of a council. It came quietly, as a friendly message from the apostles themselves. It was admirably fitted to co-operate with other influences leading in the same direction. And near the end of the fourth century, and in the early part of the fifth, the time of Augustine, it had been thus co-operating more than a hundred years; so that we need not wonder at his speaking of infant baptism as being supported by apostolic tradition.

Two eminent men of that time (near the end of the fourth century and in the early part of the fifth), Pelagius and Augustine, are now introduced by Dr. Bushnell as witnesses for infant baptism. He says, "So clear, in short, and decided was the authority of infant baptism, that Pelagius, a man of great learning, who had traveled in Britain, France, Italy, Africa Proper, Egypt and Palestine, declared, in his controversy with Augustine, about the beginning of the fifth century, that he had never heard of any impious heretic or sectary, who had denied infant baptism.' 'What,' he also asked, 'can be so impious as to hinder the baptism of infants?'"

In Augustine's animadversions on the epistle which Pelagius sent to Innocent, bishop of Rome, in his own defence (the epistle itself has been lost), we find the paragraphs relative to the subject before us; and when brought together in their proper connection, they stand thus: "Men slander me as if I denied the sacrament of baptism to infants, or promised the kingdom of heaven to some persons without the redemption of Christ; which is a thing that I never heard even any impious heretic say. For who is there so ignorant of that which is read in the gospel, as either to affirm this, or even heedlessly say such a thing, or have such a thought? In a word, who can be so impious as to hinder infants from being baptized and born again in Christ, and so make them miss of the kingdom of heaven, since our Saviour has said that none can enter into the kingdom of heaven that is not born again of water and the Holy Spirit? Who is there so impious as to refuse to an infant, of whatever age, the common redemption of mankind, and to hinder him, that is born to an uncertain life, from being born again to an everlasting and certain one?"*

We are quite willing that this testimony of Pelagius, here accurately laid before our readers in its amplest form, be estimated according to its real value. Of this they will, perhaps, be better able to judge, after hearing and examining the testimony of the remaining witness.

* See Augustine, De Peccato Originali, c. 17, etc.

"Augustine himself, also," says Dr. Bushnell, "testifies—the whole church of Christ has constantly held that infants were baptized. Infant baptism the whole church practices. It was not instituted by councils, but was ever in use.'"

We reply: Neander states that, "What Augustine found already existing in the general usage of the church, he believed might be derived either from apostolic tradition or the divine institution through general councils."* Infant baptism, it was well known, had not been instituted by any such council; and yet he seemed to find it everywhere practiced, especially in cases of special danger of death. Therefore, he inferred it must have been derived from apostolic tradition. This, in his view, was the only alternative; and, in the work claiming to be the Constitutions of the Holy Apostles, there was a command to baptize children. But, surely, there was another way in which the usage, so prevalent in his time, and far more prevalent afterwards, could have entered. And we have just seen how it could and did creep in, silently and gradually. With all his logical ingenuity and all his rhetoric, he was very liable to err in regard to the early state of the churches. He quotes largely from Cyprian's Epistle to Fidus; but, we believe, he never mentions any particular authority earlier than Cyprian. The striking remark of the historian on Origen's supposed

* Hist. of the Christian Rel. and Church, Vol. II., p. 664

reference to apostolic tradition, applies, with more than double fórce, to *Augustine's* reference, after the lapse of more than double the length of time from the days of the apostles: "An apostolic tradition—an expression, by the way, which cannot be regarded as of much weight in an age when the inclination was so strong to trace every institution which was considered of special importance to the apostles; and when so many walls of separation, hiding the freedom of prospect, had already been set up between this and the apostolic age."*

Augustine resided in the northern part of Africa. In the year 315, about forty years before his birth, a council was held at Neocæsarea, in Asia Minor, far away from Africa and all the western churches. Among the canons adopted by this council is one which was designed to remove the doubts of some in regard to the propriety of baptizing a pregnant woman, lest it might seem to involve the baptism of the child. "Concerning a woman who is pregnant [we decide] that she ought to be baptized whenever she pleases; for, in this matter, the mother communicates nothing to the child, since the deliberate purpose in the profession of faith is declared each one's own."†

From this canon we obtain a glimpse of light,

---

* Hist. of the Christ. Rel. and Church, Vol. I., p. 314.

† Περὶ κυοφορούσης ὅτι δεῖ φωτίζεσθαι ὁπότε βούλεται· οὐδὲν γὰρ ἐν τούτῳ κοινωνεῖ ἡ τίκτουσα τῷ τικτομένῳ, διὰ τὸ ἑκάστου ἰδίαν τὴν προαίρεσιν τὴν ἐπὶ τῇ ὁμολογίᾳ δείκνυσθαι.

which, perhaps, Augustine did not possess, on the state of the eastern churches in respect to baptism in the early part of the fourth century. Here it appears that, in order to be baptized, a personal profession was expected, as a matter of course, and that, in making this profession, the deliberate purpose was manifested as being each one's own. No one could answer for another, not even the mother for the child; and the child could not answer at all. The apprehension, therefore, was groundless, that the baptism of the mother, when she was overwhelmed in the water, would involve the baptism of the child, or create a case so perplexing as to render it expedient to defer the baptism of the mother till after the birth of the child. She could be baptized without delay.

Our view of the light which shines from the canon of which we have been speaking, accords with that which Grotius presents in his Annotations on the New Testament. In his note on Matt. xix: 14, he mentions this canon as being especially worthy to be noted, and adds, "For, however diversely interpreters may explain, it is manifest that the question was therefore moved concerning the baptism of the pregnant, because the child might appear to be baptized at the same time with the mother, while the custom was not to baptize any, unless upon one's own choice and profession.*

* Utcunque enim aliovorsum trahant interpretes, adparet, ideo de baptismo prægnantium motam quæstionem

In the same manner also the Greek commentators explain the principle on which the council proceeded in their decision. One of these, Balsamo, in his Compendium of Canons, says, The child cannot be baptized, because it is not yet born, and has not the deliberate purpose of the profession connected with the divinely appointed baptism.* And another, Zonaras, with equal clearness, expresses himself thus: The embryo needs baptism when it shall be able to have the deliberate purpose.†

In the year 325, at the council of Nice, Eusebius, the ecclesiastical historian, prepared a document for the signature of the three hundred and eighteen bishops who were there, and read it in the presence of Constantine the Great, and of the whole council. It is preserved in the Greek original, both by Socrates and by Theodoret, in their ecclesiastical histories; and in it Eusebius says, "As we have received from the bishops that were before us, *both in the previous catechetical instruction, and also when we received the laver;* as we have learned from the divine Scriptures, and as, in the presbytery itself, and also in the episcopate, we have believed and taught, so also now believing,

---

quod videretur cum matre simul proles baptizari, quæ tamen baptizari non soleret, nisi super propria voluntate ac professione. Vol. I., p. 385, ed. 1755.

* Οὐ δύναται φωτισθῆναι διὰ τὸ μηκέτι εἰς φῶς ἐλθεῖν, μηδὲ προαίρεσιν ἔχειν τῆς ὁμολογίας τοῦ θείου βαπτίσματος.

† Τὸ ἔμβρυον χρήζει βαπτίσματος ὅτε προαιρεῖσθαι δυνήσαται.

we set forth our belief, and it is this: We believe," etc.*

Here the important fact is incidentally disclosed that, not only Eusebius himself, but also the other bishops assembled in that great council, had received instruction before they were baptized; and most of them, unquestionably, had been born of Christian parents.

About forty years after the close of the eighth century, the learned Walafrid Strabo, at the request of Reginbert, wrote a book on the Beginnings and Additions in Ecclesiastical Affairs.† It is pronounced by Cardinal Bellarmine to be a useful work.‡ It was printed at Cologne in 1568. It may be found also in the fifteenth volume of the great collection published at Lyons in 1677.§ It consists of thirty-one chapters. The twenty-sixth treats of Baptism, and begins thus: "Concerning Baptism also some things are to be said. What was clearly prefigured in the passage of the Red Sea and of the Jordan, but

---

* *Καθὼς παρελάβομεν παρὰ τῶν πρὸ ἡμῶν ἐπισκόπων, καὶ τῇ πρώτῃ κατηχήσει καὶ ὅτε καὶ τὸ λουτρὸν ἐλαμβάνομεν*, &c. See Socrates, B. I, c. 8, and Theodoret B. I., c. 12. See also a fair and faithful translation by Dr. Cave, in his *Lives of the Fathers*, Vol. II., p. 112, Oxford, 1840; or in the Historical Essay, preliminary to the work entitled *Memorials of Baptist Martyrs*, Am. Bap. Pub. Soc.

† De Exordiis et Incrementis Rerum Ecclesiasticarum.

‡ De Scrip. Eccles.

§ Maxima Bibliotheca Veterum Patrum et antiquorum Scriptorum Ecclesiasticorum.

more obscurely prefigured by many other figures, is here made known. This to those who were converted to faith in the Messiah, was in the beginning of the new grace first shown by John to have been provided, not by his own invention, but by divine constitution; as he himself testifies, saying, He who sent me to baptize in water," etc. After some other remarks, the following statements are made:

"It is to be noted that in primitive times, the grace of baptism was accustomed to be given only to those who, in body and mind, had come to such maturity as to be able to know and understand what benefit is to be obtained in baptism, what is to be professed, and what to be believed, and, finally, what is to be preserved by the new-born in Christ. Indeed the venerable Father Augustine, in the book of his Confessions, relates concerning himself, that he continued a catechumen almost to the age of twenty-five years, with the intention that, through this delay, he, instructed distinctly on each subject, might be led to choose freely for himself, and the ardent passions of the slippery age cooling off, he might be better able to preserve what was to be obtained in baptism.

"But, diligence in the divine religion increasing, —the lovers of Christian dogmatics understanding that the original sin of Adam holds liable to punishment, not only those who by their own deeds have increased the transgression, but even those who are without any deeds of their own (because, according to the Psalmist, they are conceived and born in iniquities, they cannot be free from sin, while they proceed from a corrupt root; so that deservedly concerning all that is said by the apostle, 'all have sinned, and come short of the glory of God,' and concerning Adam, 'In whom all have sinned),; This, therefore, the followers of the sound faith perceiving [took care] that the little ones be baptized for the remission of sins, lest they perish, if they die without the remedy of the grace of regeneration. Not, as certain heretics, opposing the grace of God, contended that children are baptized by no necessity, because they have not yet sinned. If this were true, either they were not to be baptized, or if they were baptized unnecessarily, then imperfect and not true in them was the sacrament of baptism, which, in the creed, we confess to be given for the remission of sins. Therefore, because all whom the grace of God does not liberate, perish in original sin, children are necessarily baptized, even those who have not added to it by their own evil deeds. Which also Saint Augustine shows in his book on the Baptism of Children, and the African Councils and innumerable documents of other Fathers testify."*

* Notandum quod, primis temporibus, illis solummodo baptismi gratiam dari solitam qui et corporis et mentis integritate jam ad hoc pervenerant, ut scire et intelligere possunt quid emolumenti in baptismo consequendum, quid confidendum atque credendum, quid postremo renatis in Christo esset servandum, etc.

These paragraphs need no comment. They come from a source which cannot be suspected of any partiality in our favor; and yet it will be perceived at once that they confirm the representations which we have made. They come from a zealous supporter of infant baptism; and yet they affirm, as an unquestionable historical fact, in the presence of catholic Christendom, that, in the primitive times, infants were not baptized, and, of course, that for infant baptism there could have been no genuine tradition from the apostles. They come from a staunch friend of Augustine; and yet they show that his strong language, seeming to assert the universality of infant baptism, must be received with some abatement; for they incidentally present evidence from his own pen, that even he himself was not baptized in his infancy, although it is well known his mother was distinguished for her Christian piety and her deep solicitude for his spiritual welfare. That a large abatement of this kind must be made, appears also from other statements of Augustine himself, to say nothing of evidence independent of these. In his fourteenth sermon on the Words of the Apostles, he speaks of its being a common thing to inquire respecting a Christian's child, Is he a catechumen or a believer? That is, is he still receiving preparatory instruction, or has he been baptized as a believer? To say that it was common to have occasion to make such an inquiry is equivalent to saying that it was common for children to be instructed before being baptized.

The reduction of the practice of baptizing instructed children to the practice of baptizing children too young to be instructed, or to answer for themselves, was gradual. It was facilitated in various ways, and urged on by imperative considerations; but still it had obstacles to overcome. Augustine still had occasion to answer some hard questions on the subject. Of these we present a single specimen. The established baptismal service, when applied to infants, seemed to some intelligent and conscientious persons to be inconsistent with the great principle of common veracity. This is brought distinctly to view in Augustine's reply to Boniface, a contemporary bishop.

"You seem to yourself," he says, "to have proposed a most difficult question indeed, at the close of your inquiry. With the carefulness, manifestly, with which you are accustomed to be exceedingly on your guard against a falsehood,* you say, 'If I set before you an infant, and ask you whether, when he grows up, he will be a chaste man? or whether he will be a thief? your answer doubtless will be, I cannot tell; and, whether he in that infant age has any good or evil thought? You will say, I know not. Since, therefore, you dare not say any thing either concerning his future behavior or his present thoughts, why is it that, when they are brought to baptism, their

* Difficillimam sane quæstionem tibi proposuisse visus es in extremo inquisitionis tuae: ea videlicet intentione qua soles vehementer cavere mendacium.

parents, as sponsors for them, answer and say that they do what that age can have no thought of; or, if they have, nobody knows what they are? For we ask those by whom they are brought, and say, 'Does he believe in God? concerning that age which has no knowledge whether there is a God or not. They answer, He does believe; and in like manner answers are made to all the rest; so that I wonder how the parents do in those matters answer so confidently for the child, that he does this or that good thing which the baptizer demands at the time of his baptism; and yet, if at the same time I ask, Will this baptized person prove chaste? or not prove a thief? I question whether any dare so answer, He will, or will not be such or such a one, and they answer without hesitation, He does believe in God, and he does turn to God.' Then at the close, you add, 'I entreat you to give me a short answer to these questions, in such a manner as that you do not urge to me the prescription or the customariness of the thing, but give me the reason of it.'

"When I had read your letter over and over, and had considered it as far as my short time would allow, it made me call to mind my friend Nebridius, who being a very diligent and sagacious inquirer into matters that were obscure, especially such as concern religion, could not endure a short answer to a weighty question, and took it very ill if any one desired such a thing; and would with an angry voice and look reprimand him, if he were a person that might be so used, as counting him unfit to ask such questions, who did not consider how much might and ought to be said on so great a matter. But I am not angry with you, as he was accustomed to be; for you are a bishop occupied with many cares, as I also am; so that neither have you the leisure to read a long discourse, nor I to write one; for he being then a young man, that would not be answered in brief to such things, made many inquiries in conversation with me, and inquired as one at leisure from one that was so too; but you, considering now your own circumstances that ask, and mine that am asked, bid me answer briefly about so great a matter; and this I here do as well as I can. The Lord assist me that I may be able to satisfy your demand.

"We often express ourselves so, that when Good Friday is nigh, we say, To-morrow, or, The day after to-morrow is our Lord's passion; though it is a great many years ago that he suffered, and his passion was never performed but once. So on the Lord's Day we say, This day our Lord arose; though since he arose it is so many years. Why is there nobody so silly as to say we lie when we speak so, but for this reason; because we give names to those days, from the representation which they make to us of those on which the things were indeed done; so that *that* is called the very day which is not the very day, but answers to it in the revolution of time; and that which is not done on that day, but was done a long time ago, is spoken of as done on that day, because the sacrament of it is then celebrated. Was not Christ in his own person offered up once for all? And yet in the sacrament he is offered up, not only every Easter, but every day; nor does he lie, who, being asked, says he is offered up. For sacraments could not be sacraments if they had not a resemblance of those things of which they are the sacraments; and from this resemblance they commonly have the names of the things themselves.

"As therefore the sacrament of Christ's body is after a certain fashion Christ's body; and the sacrament of Christ's blood is Christ's blood, so the sacrament of faith is faith. But to believe is nothing else than to have faith. And so when it is responded that an infant believes, who has not yet the faculty of faith, it is responded that he has faith on account of the sacrament of faith; and that he turns to God, on account of the sacrament of conversion; because the response also itself pertains to the celebration of the sacrament. So the apostle on this same subject of baptism says, 'We are buried together with Christ by baptism into death.' He does not say, We signify a burial; but he uses the word itself, We are buried; so that he calls the sacrament of so great a thing by the name of the thing itself.

"And so an infant, though he be not yet constituted a believer (fidelis) by that faith which consists in the will of believers, yet he is by the sacrament of that faith; for, as he is said to believe, so he is called a believer; not from his having the thing itself in his mind, but from his receiving the sacrament of it. And when a person begins to have a sense of these things, he does not repeat that sacrament, but understands the force of it, and by the consent of will squares himself to the true meaning of it; and till he can do this, the sacrament will avail to his preservation against all contrary powers, and so far it will avail that if he depart this life before the use of reason, he will by this Christian remedy of the sacrament itself (the charity of the church recommending him) be made free from that condemnation which by one man entered into the world. He that does not believe this, and thinks it cannot be done, is actually an infidel, though he has the sacrament of faith; and that infant is much better who, though he has not faith in his mind, yet puts no bar of a contrary mind against it, and so receives the sacrament to his soul's health.

"I have given such an answer to your questions as, I suppose is, to ignorant and contentious people, not enough; and to understanding and quiet people perhaps more than enough. Nor have I, to spare my pains, urged to you the custom's being so firmly established; but I have, as well as I could, explained to you the reason of that most beneficial custom."

The ingenious sophistry of this reply, it is probable, will be more manifest to most of our readers than it was to Augustine himself. Indeed he may not have perceived it at all. But they will readily perceive that if the sacrament of faith constitutes the child a believer, then, to ask, Does this child believe? is to ask, Has this child received the sacrament of faith? while this is the very thing which he, not having received, is now brought for the purpose of obtaining. The question is asked, and must be satisfactorily answered, before the baptism, the sacrament of faith, can be administered. The only way to conceal the absurd and absolute preposterousness of asking the question, is to acknowledge duplicity in making the response, that is, to suppose that in the question, believing means *one* thing, and that in the response, it means *another!*

The manner in which Augustine denounces as an infidel every one in the church who was not convinced of the propriety of the dominant practice commended by him, is very striking. We allude to the following passage near the close of the reply: "He that does not believe this [what was affirmed to be accomplished in connection with infant baptism] is actually an infidel, though he has the sacrament of faith." From this severe rebuke, as well as from other evidence, it appears that there were such persons who, in his estimation, needed to be rebuked; and, in pronouncing sentence on these, a friendly warning might be given indirectly to the prudence of his friend Boniface, the bishop to whom he was writing. That there were such persons in the church appears also, and still more clearly, from a parallel passage in his work on the Deserts and Remission of Sins and the

Baptism of Children. There referring to our Saviour's words in John iii : 19, he asks, Whence does he say, 'Light is come into the world,' unless he says it concerning his advent, without the sacrament of which advent how are children said to be in the light? Or how do not those persons have even this in the love of darkness, who, as they themselves do not believe [but are actually infidels] *so neither think that their children are to be baptized*, when they fear for them the death of the body ?*

It is painful and humiliating to think of the errors into which even good and great men are liable to fall; and it is instructive to see how they sometimes unconsciously deceive themselves and others. Here the mild and monitory words of Neander may be called to mind with benefit to us all. They are worthy of perpetual remembrance. "Augustine," he remarks, "assumed as that on which faith must fix—*every thing given in the tradition of the church*; hence he was led to admit many foreign elements; and his well exercised, speculative and dialectic intellect made it easy for him to find reasons for

* De Peccatorum Meritis et Remissione et de Baptismo Parvulorum, Lib. I., cap XXXIII. (61.) Works, Tom. X., p. 35. Ben. ed. Unde, *Lux venit in mundum*, nisi de suo dicit adventu, sine cujus adventus sacramento quomodo parvuli esse dicuntur in luce? Aut quomodo non et hoc in dilectione tenebrarum habent, qui quemadmodum ipsi non credunt, *sic nec baptizandos suos parvulos, arbitrantur*, quando eis mortem corporis timent?

every thing. His system of faith wanted that historical and critical direction, whereby alone, returning back, at all periods of time, to the pure and original fountain of Christianity, it could make and preserve itself free from foreign elements which continually threaten to mix in with the current of impure temporal tradition."*

* Hist. of Christ. Rel. and Church, Vol. II, p. 359.

VI.

INFANT BAPTISM AND INFANT COMMUNION.

WE now request our readers to weigh carefully and candidly the evidence which has been laid before them. The question to be decided is one of no trivial import. Is Infant Baptism a divine institute, established by our Lord? or is it an unauthorized device of men? Was it known and sanctioned in the days of the apostles, or was it introduced afterwards? Is it a part of pure and primitive Christianity, or is it a corruption, a departure from the simplicity that is in Christ, an expedient resorted to under the overpowering influence of erroneous impressions in regard to the efficacy of the baptismal act, and in regard to its necessity in order to any one's being admitted into heaven?

Similar questions might be asked also concerning Infant Communion, which came into use along with Infant Baptism.

From time immemorial, a participation in the Lord's Supper had been regarded as one of the privileges of the baptized. Infant Communion made its first appearance where Infant Baptism first appeared, namely, in the African churches, and the first mention of it occurs in the writings of Cyprian, the zealous and powerful advocate for the baptism of endangered children in their earliest infancy, about the middle of the third century. In his collection of testimonies addressed to Quirinus,* he teaches the necessity of being baptized, from John iii : 5; "Except a man be born again, of water and the Spirit, he cannot enter into the kingdom of God;" and the necessity of partaking of the Lord's Supper, from John vi : 53; "Except ye eat of the flesh of the Son of man, and drink his blood, ye shall not have life in you."

In his Treatise on the Lapsed, he sets forth the guilt of those who had voluntarily participated in the heathen sacrifices, and says (c. 7): "Many, however, were unsatisfied with doing destruction upon themselves; men were urged to their ruin by mutual encouragements, and the fatal cup of death was offered from mouth to mouth. That nothing might be wanting to their load of guilt, even infants in their parents' arms, carried or led, were deprived while yet tender of what was granted them in the commencement of life.† Will not these children in the day of judgment say, We did no sin; it was not our will to hasten from the bread and cup of the Lord to an unhallowed pollution. We perish through unfaithfulness not our own; and our parents on earth

* B. III., c. 25 and c. 26.

† Infantes quoque parentum manibus, vel impositi vel attracti, amiserunt provuli quod in primo statim nativitatia exordio fuerant consecuti.

have robbed us of the parentage in heaven; they forfeited for us the Church as a Mother, and God as a Father; and thus while young and unaware, and ignorant of that grievous act, we are included in a league of sin by others, and perish through their deceit."

In c. 16, he makes the following statement: "Listen to an event that took place in my own presence, and on my own testimony. Some parents who made their escape, in the thoughtlessness of terror left behind them at nurse an infant daughter, whom the nurse finding in her hands gave over to the magistrates. Unable through its tender years to eat flesh, they gave it, before an idol to which the crowd assembled, bread mingled with some wine, which, however, was the remains of that which had been used in the soul-slaughter of perishing Christians. The mother afterwards got back her child, but the infant was unable to express and make known the act that had been committed, as she had before been to understand or prevent it. Through ignorance, therefore, it arose, that when we were sacrificing the mother brought it in with her. The child, however, mixed with the holy congregation, could not bear our prayers and worship; it was at one moment convulsed with weeping, then became tossed like a wave by throbs of feeling, and the babe's soul, yet in the tender days, confessed a consciousness of what had happened with what signs it could, as if forced to do so by a torturer. When, however, after the solemnities were complete, the deacon began to offer the cup to those who were there, and, in the course of their receiving, its turn came, the little child turned its face away, under the instinct of God's majesty, compressed its lips in resistance, and refused the cup. The deacon, however, persevered and forced upon her, against her will, of the sacrament of the cup. There followed a sobbing and vomiting. The eucharist was not able to remain in a body and mouth that had been polluted. The draught, which had been consecrated in the blood of the Lord, made its way from a body which had been desecrated. So great is the power of the Lord, so great the majesty. The secrets of the darkness are laid open under his sight, and God's priest could not be deceived in crimes however hidden. Thus much concerning an infant which had not the age to make known a crime which was committed on her by the act of others."

After these singular disclosures, we need not be surprised at the unequivocal statement of the highest authority in ecclesiastical history, that, "as the Church of North Africa was the first to bring prominently into notice the necessity of infant baptism, so in connection with this they introduced also the communion of infants."*

Ages passed away; and sometimes in a single age

* Neander's Hist. of the Christ. Rel. and Church, translated by Torrey. Vol I., p. 333.

great changes occur. Ages passed away, and, in the meantime, the various influences and pressing considerations which had introduced infant baptism and infant communion, continued to extend and confirm these practices more and more.

After the lapse of nearly two hundred years, Augustine, in one of his works,* says: "Let us hear the Lord, speaking, not indeed concerning the sacrament of the laver, but concerning the sacrament of his holy table, to which no one, unless baptized, rightly approaches: Unless ye eat my flesh, and drink my blood, ye shall not have life in you.† Why do we inquire further? What can be replied to this? . . . . Will any one dare to say that this sentence does not pertain to children, and that they can have life in themselves without partaking of his body and blood: because he does not say, 'He that has not eaten,' as concerning baptism, 'He that is not born again:' but says, 'If ye shall not eat,' as addressing those who were able to hear and understand, which, undoubtedly, little children are not able to do."

In a sermon he remarks: "Infants they are, but they receive his sacraments; infants they are, but they are made partakers of his table."‡ In the work

* De Peccatorum Meritis et Remissione, et de Baptismo Parvulorum. Lib. I. cap. xx: 26 and 27. Works, Tom. x: col. 15. Ben. ed.

† John vi: 53.

‡ Serm. 174. De Verbis Apostoli, 1 Tim. 1. Works, Tom. V., col. 834. Ben. ed.

first quoted, he also says: "Most excellently the Carthaginian Christians call baptism itself nothing else than salvation, and the sacrament of the body of Christ nothing else than life. Whence is this, unless from ancient, as I think, and apostolic tradition, by which the churches of Christ hold, as a fixed fact, that without baptism and *participation of the Lord's table*, no one of mankind can come either to the kingdom of God or to salvation and eternal life?" *

And in one of his epistles he expresses himself in the following decisive manner: "No one who remembers that he is a Christian of the catholic faith denies, or doubts, that children unbaptized and not having partaken of the Lord's body and blood, have not life in themselves, and thus are exposed to eternal punishment."†

Innocent, bishop of Rome in the time of Augustine,

---

* Optime Punici Christiani baptismum ipsum nihil aliud quam salutem et sacramentum corporis Christi, nihil aliud quam vitam vocant. Unde, nisi ex antiqua, ut existimo, et apostolica traditione, qua ecclesiæ Christi insitum tenent, præter baptismum et participationem mensæ Dominicæ, non solum ad regnum Dei, sed nec ad salutem et vitam æternam posse quemquam hominum pervenire? See Lib I., cap. xxiv., 34. Works, Tom. x., col. 19. Ben. ed.

† Epist. 106. Nullus qui meminit Catholicæ fidei Christianum negat aut dubitat parvulos, nec recepta gratia regenerationis in Christo, sine cibo carnis ejus et sanguinis potu, non habere in se vitam, ac per hoc pœnæ sempiternæ obnoxius.

maintained the necessity of infant communion from John vi : 53.*

Gelasius, also bishop of Rome about a century later, did the same.†

About the same time—the end of the fifth century and the beginning of the sixth—the author of the Greek works ascribed to Dionysius the Areopagite (mentioned in Acts xvii : 34), speaks of infant communion together with infant baptism, as an established usage.‡ He was supposed to have been ordained Bishop of Athens by the Apostle Paul; and his writings had very great influence. They were translated into Latin; and from the ninth century they were widely circulated in the Latin or Roman Catholic Church. At length, however, about the middle of the fifteenth century, their spuriousness was detected by Laurentius Valla.§

Near the close of the sixth century (590–604) the Pope St. Gregory the Great, in his book of Sacraments, treating of the baptism of infants, says: "Who are not prohibited from nursing before the sacred communion, if it be necessary."

In the seventh century, the Council of Toledo (Concilium Toletanum XI.), A.D. 675, excused from ecclesiastical censure those by whom the bread in

---

* In literis ad Patres Synodi Milevitanæ.

† In Epistola ad Episcopos per Picenum.

‡ De Ecclesiastica Hierarchia, c. VII.

§ See Gieseler's Ecclesiastical History, Vol. II., p. 80.

the eucharist was rejected through extreme sickness or in infancy, when they knew not what they did.

A few years before the close of the eight century (A.D. 790), the Emperor Charlemagne speaks of infants washed with the water of baptism, and satiated with the food of the Lord's body and the drinking of his blood.* In his Laws,† it is ordered that the presbyter always have the eucharist prepared, so that when any one sickens, *or a child is weak*, he may administer the sacrament to him immediately, lest he die without the communion.

The *Ordo Romanus*, composed in the ninth century, gives the following direction: "Concerning children care is to be taken, lest, after they shall have been baptized, they receive any food or nurse, without the greatest necessity, before they partake of the sacrament of Christ's body."

Paschasius Radbert, a little before the middle of the ninth century, wrote an extensive work on the Lord's Supper. In this work, with a startling boldness, he expounded and defended the doctrine of transubstantiation; and, at the same time, he maintained that baptized infants, even if they should die before participating in the holy supper, would be saved in consequence of their union with Christ by baptism. Controversy ensued, and it was continued for ages. The opinion that in the eucharist the bread is changed

---

* Lib. II. De Imaginibus, c. 27.

† Collected by Ansegisus, Lib. I., c. 161.

into the body and the wine into the blood of our Lord, prevailed more and more, especially after the council at Rome in 1079.

William De Champeaux, Bishop of Chalons, an intimate friend of St. Bernard, taught, as Bossuet expresses it, 'that he who receives one kind alone receives Jesus Christ entire.'*

Hugo à St. Victor, at Paris, who died about the year 1141, maintained that in the eucharist wine alone might be given to infants, because under each kind, whether bread or wine, the body and blood of Christ is at the same time received.† He pursued a middle course in respect to the necessity of infant communion. For, regarding the custom of the ancient church, he taught that the eucharist was indeed to be given to children, under the form of wine; but with caution and limitation. For, if in preserving the blood of Christ, or in administering it to children, there is danger [of accident to the sacred element], the observance should rather be omitted. Then he says that there is to the children no peril of salvation if they should depart without the communion, because they are already made members of Christ by baptism. Lanfranc, Archbishop of Canterbury, taught the same. Hugo, in his work on the Sacraments, adds

* Que qui reçoit une seule espèce, reçoit Jésus-Christ tout entier.

† See J. Bona, Rerum Liturgicarum, Lib. II., c. 18, § 1, p. 723.

with respect to infants, "The sacrament in the form of blood is to be administered by the finger of the priest, because such are naturally able to suck."*

Paschal II., who was Pope from 1099 to 1118, wrote an epistle (32) to Pontius, Abbot of Clugny, in which he orders that children, and the feeble who cannot absorb the bread, may communicate in the blood alone, deeming this more becoming than to permit a dipped communion.† He commanded to give the two symbols separately, except to those who were extremely sick and to *little infants, whom he permitted to communicate with the wine.* After his time, this continued to be the usage of the Western or Romish Church, in regard to infants, so long as infant communion was practiced.‡

In the twelfth century, Odo, Bishop of Paris, who was alive in 1175, commanded his presbyters not to give the elements to children in any manner.§

* De Sacramentis et Ceremoniis Ecclesiasticis, Lib. I. c. 20. Idem sacramentum in specie sanguinis est ministrandum digito sacerdotis, quia tales naturaliter sugere possunt.

† See J. Bona, Rerum Liturgicarum, Lib. II., c. 18, § 3, 719. Ut parvuli et infirmi, qui panem absorbere non possunt, in solo sanguine communicent, hoc decentius existimans quam intinctam communionem permittere.

‡ Paschal's Epistle entire is inserted by Baronius, in his Ecclesiastical Annals, in connection with the year 1118, n. 3. See it also in J. Schilterus, De Libertate Ecclesiarum Germanicarum, Lib. IV., c. 5, § 3.

§ See his Synodal Statutes, c. 39.

Thus in the Gallican Church, the custom of communicating the little ones ceased in the twelfth century; a custom which Hugo à Victor, a writer of the same century, wished to restore, yet affirms to have ceased, in his time, though some vestiges of it still remained. In some Roman Catholic countries vestiges of it remained long after his time.*

In the sixteenth century, when the great Lutheran Reformation occurred, and there was earnest inquiry on many religious subjects, the Romish Church, at the Council of Trent, decreed 'that children are not obligated to the sacramental communion,' as follows:

"Session 21st (the 5th under the Supreme Pontiff, Pius IV.), July 16, 1562.

"Doctrine concerning communion, under each kind, and of children.

"The holy ecumenical and general council at Trent, in the Holy Spirit legitimately assembled, the same legates of the Apostolic See presiding, since concerning the tremendous and most holy sacrament of the eucharist, in divers places, by the arts of the most wicked demon, various monsters of errors are circulated, on account of which in some provinces many seem to have departed from the faith of the

* For ample evidence of this, see Zornii Historia Eucharistiæ Infantum, ex Antiquitatibus Ecclesiarum tum Occidentalium tum Orientalium secundum decem Sæculorum seriem et multiplicem varietatem illustrata,—printed at Berlin, in 1736; a work to which we are indebted for its lucid presentation of many important facts.

Catholic Church and from obedience, has resolved that those things which pertain to communion under each kind, and of children, be in this place expounded. Wherefore it interdicts to all the faithful of Christ, and forbids that hereafter they dare either to believe or to preach, otherwise than is in these decrees set forth and defined."

. . . .

"CAN. IV.—*That children are not obligated to Sacramental Communion.*

"Finally, the same holy council teaches that children wanting the use of reason are by no necessity obligated to the sacramental communion of the eucharist; if regenerated by the laver of baptism and incorporated in Christ, they cannot in that age lose the already obtained grace of the sons of God. Yet neither is antiquity therefore to be condemned, if in some places it has sometimes observed this custom. For as those most holy fathers have had, according to the state of that time, probable cause for what they did, so certainly, it is to be believed, without controversy, that they did it by no necessity of salvation."

Appended to this canon is the following:

"If any one shall say that the communion of the eucharist is necessary to children before they come to years of discretion, let him be anathema."*

---

* See p. 109–111, Canones et decreta Concilii Tridentini, ex editione Romana A.D. 1834, Leipsic, 1853. Sessio xxi.

In the catechism of the Council of Trent, published by command of Pope Pius V., an octavo volume of more than five hundred pages, these remarks are made, namely: "The Council of Lateram [in 1215]

---

quæ est quinta sub Pio IV. Pont. Max. celebrata die xvi. mensis Julii, MDLXII.

Doctrina de communione sub utroque specie et parvulorum.

Sacro Sancta œccumencia et generalis Tridentina synodus in Spiritu Sancto legitime congregata, præsidentibus in ea eisdem apostolicæ sedis legatis, quum de tremendo et sanctissimo eucharistiæ sacramento varia diversis in locis errorum monstra nequissimi dæmonis artibus circumferentur, ob quæ in nonnullis provinciis multi a catholicæ ecclesiæ fide atque obedientia videantur discessisse, censuit ea, quæ ad communionem sub utraque specie et parvulorum pertinent, hoc loco exponenda esse. Quapropter cunctis Christi fidelibus interdicit, ne posthac de iis aliter vel credere, vel docere vel prædicare audeant, quam est his decretis explicatum atque definitum.

. . . .

CAN. IV. *Parvulos non obligari ad communionem sacramentalem.*

Denique eadem sancta synodus docet parvulos usu rationis carentes nulla obligari necessitate ad sacramentalem eucharistiæ communionem, siquidem per baptismi lavacrum regenerati et Christo incorporati adeptam jam filiorum Dei gratiam in illa ætate amittere non possunt. Neque ideo tamen damnanda est antiquitas, si eum morem in quibusdam locis aliquando servavit. Ut enim sanctissimi illi Patres sui facti probabilem causam pro illius temporis ratione habuerunt, ita certe eos nulla salutis necessitate id fecisse sine controversia credendum est.

Appended to Can. iv. Si quis dixerit, parvulis, antequam

decreed that all the faithful should communicate, at least once a year, at Easter, and that the omission should be chastised by exclusion from the society of the faithful. But although this law, sanctioned, as it is, by the authority of God, and of his church, regards all the faithful, the pastor, however, will teach that it does not extend to persons who have not arrived at the years of discretion, because they are incapable of discerning the Holy Eucharist from common food, and cannot bring with them to this sacrament the piety and devotion which it demands. To extend the precept to them would appear inconsistent with the institution of this sacrament by our Lord: 'Take,' says he, 'and eat;' words which cannot apply to infants, who are evidently incapable of taking and eating. In some places, it is true, an ancient practice prevailed of giving the Holy Eucharist even to infants; but, for the reasons already assigned, and for other reasons most consonant to Christian piety, this practice has been long discontinued, by authority of the same church.*

Among the "other reasons" alluded to, the following might be mentioned: 1. Because infant communion has no firm foundation in the word of God.

---

ad annos discretionis pervenerint, necessarium esse eucharistiæ communionem : anathema sit.

* P. 227. The Catechism is translated into English by the Rev. J. Donovan, Professor, etc., of the Royal College, at Maynooth.

2. Because, especially, it is not required in John vi: 53, but the declaration of Christ there made concerning the spiritual reception of himself by faith, had been misinterpreted and badly distorted from the genuine sense to the reception of the sacrament 3. Because it is not necessary in order to obtain salvation. 4. Because it is an unreasonable service, and a needless stumbling-block to our natural sense of propriety. 5. Because in being forced upon infants it is liable to be the occasion of hurtful and scandalous accidents to the body and blood of Christ, and thus dishonor him, and bring reproach on the holy ordinance. 6. Because infants cannot examine themselves, and, discerning the Lord's body, partake of it in remembrance of him, according to 1 Cor. xi: 24–29.

The Oriental churches still adhere to infant communion. Fourteen or fifteen years ago, the Pope, Pius IX., by an encyclical or circular letter, in the modern Greek language, exhorted them to return to the Roman Church. Among the replies which this document called forth from the Greek Church one of the ablest, that of Alexander de Stourdza, of Edessa, has recently been translated into English and published in the *Christian Review*. The author observes: "Our Lord, the High Priest and spotless victim, said expressly to his disciples, as he presented to them the cup of the New Testament, 'drink ye all of it.' Now since the sacrament of the body and blood of Jesus Christ was instituted for a perpetual observance, even 'until he come,' and since our

Saviour has said, 'except ye eat the flesh of the Son of man and drink his blood, ye have no life in you,' the Eastern Church, faithful to primitive example, has never dared to withhold the cup from the laity, *nor even from infants of tender age.* She ordains, moreover, that the bread shall be drenched in the consecrated wine."* . . . Alluding to the decree of the Council of Trent, he adds: "The churches of the west have condemned an immense majority of the human race to die before they have tasted of the bread of life! They may accumulate the most specious arguments in favor of this practice; but these arguments will never be able to stand before the right and simple faith, before the authority of the universal church of all times. Let them beware! By reasoning in this way they will by little come at last to *allow only the baptism of adults.*"

Here we pause. From the point of observation at which we have arrived, let us look around and survey some of the singular sights which have been disclosed as successive generations of men have appeared, and have passed rapidly away.

In the dim distance of far more than a thousand years, stand St. Cyprian and St. Augustine, affirming the necessity of infant communion, and proving it

---

* In the Greek Church, the bread sodden in the wine is given to the communicant, from the cup, with a spoon. This fact is stated by the translator, the Rev. Dr. Arnold, who resided several years as a missionary at Athens.

from the words of our Saviour in John vi : 53, "Except ye eat the body of the Son of man, and drink his blood, ye have no life in you." Other bishops, yes, bishops of Rome, too, and bishops of the distant East, echo the same. It is recognized by ecclesiastical mandates, and by imperial laws. At length circumstances somewhat change. New thoughts are suggested. Discussions arise. New influences are felt. Considerations that had been overlooked are appreciated. The words of our Saviour, that had been misunderstood and wrongly applied, are correctly interpreted. And motives pure, and, probably, motives mixed with human frailty and error, combine, under the overruling providence of God, to produce a most remarkable result. What St. Cyprian and St. Augustine had affirmed on this subject was condemned and anathematized! condemned and anathematized by the general council at Trent, with the sanction of him who claimed to be the universal Bishop, the Vicar and Vicegerent of Jesus Christ on earth, and with the practical concurrence of all the Protestant Churches!

Henceforth let no man despair of other changes in the right direction. But how shall the great ecclesiastical controversies be rightly terminated? The Greek and other eastern churches do not acknowledge the authority of the Romish and other western churches. *But the word of the Lord endureth forever.* While both the great anti-Protestant portions of Christendom assail each other, and urge their antagonistic claims to apostolic tradition and primitive usage, let us, thankful to God for the unerring rule of faith and practice which he has given us, endeavor to understand and obey it, and set an attractive example by yielding joyfully the lovely fruits of obedience.

The same arguments, for the most part, that disprove and forbid infant communion, disprove and forbid infant baptism. And if infant communion is a great error, infant baptism is a still greater error, and more pernicious. Infant communion does not deprive the child of the benefits of communion when he arrives at the age of discretion. But infant baptism, performed in his early infancy, does, so far as it is regarded, prevent his ever receiving the benefit of *being baptized upon a deliberate profession of his faith*, an event which he ought to be able to remember, amidst the temptations and cares of life, till he descends into his grave with the well-assured hope of a glorious resurrection.

Infant baptism not only thus wrongs the child, and takes from him what belongs to him, and was designed for his use when he becomes a believer, but it wrongs our Lord himself. It actually, though not intentionally, sets aside his authority. It perverts an ordinance which he saw fit to appoint, and applies it to those to whom it is not adapted, and to whom he did not intend to have it applied. It tends, in effect, to annul what he ordained. He instituted baptism for professing disciples only. The apostles sanctioned no other. The Bible not only gives no support to infant baptism, but it has passages which clearly show that infants were not baptized in the time of the apostles. And the earliest ecclesiastical history after the time of the apostles knows nothing of the practice. It is a practice that originated in error; in a sad misunderstanding of John iii: 5, and other passages; in confounding the sign with the thing signified; in attributing a mysterious efficacy to the act of baptism; and in a commendable parental affection, misguided, and mingled with the surrounding superstition. It came as an angel of light, to perform a work of mercy. But, angel of light as it seemed to be, it has done an immensity of evil. Alas, what multitudes have been deceived with the vain confidence of being regenerate, and made heirs of eternal life, by an external act performed on them in a state of unconsciousness, or have been led to think that, in connection with such an act, their salvation has, somehow, been secured!

No beautiful association of parental duties and parental confidence in God, unutterably important as these are in their places—no ingenious fiction of a presumptive faith, strong and precious as the agencies and influences of faithful and judicious parents are upon their children—no plausible apology whatever can justify the virtual annulling of the initiatory ordinance which our Lord, in his wisdom and love, established for the observance of his disciples.

Infant baptism led to infant communion. Infant communion, the comparatively innocent accomplice, has been convicted and condemned. Shall the principal offender be permitted to escape condemnation? Why should this seeming angel of light still be caressed and lauded? Why should theological or metaphysical, or any pretentious theories, be constructed to keep up a lamentable influence, ill-gotten at first, and too long retained. No good reason can be given. Infant baptism has been proved to be, not an ordinance instituted by our Lord, or authorized by his apostles, or known to their earliest successors, but a human device, at a later period—the offspring of misapprehension and of ill-directed kindness, relying on the supposed saving efficacy of a religious ceremony. Whatever may be said of past ages, the present can have no valid excuse for continuing to maintain the error which we are deploring. The present state of Christendom is summoning us to conflicts and to trials of our faith, in which we have special need of being established and built up, not in error, but in the truth. How else can we satisfy our own consciences? How else can we meet successfully the Romanists and the Greeks, with their misleading traditions, or rescue from infidelity the sceptics, stumbling over our inconsistencies?

The sacraments, baptism and the Lord's supper, have in themselves no efficacy; but the recipient, in order to be benefited by them, must receive them with faith in Christ. This, one of the great principles for which we have always contended, has now come to be generally conceded by persons of evangelical views in other communions. "But," as it has been said, with an alarming truthfulness, "until infant baptism be openly abandoned, there is a constant tendency to re-action, a danger of relapse. The entering wedge for the recurrence of all that is most fatal in the delusions of Popery is in the crevice, and a few hard blows may at any moment split all other Protestantism to pieces. It is not, therefore, merely in regard to the time and circumstances of a ceremony that Baptists are contending, but it is for *principles* the most valuable of any embodied in the Reformation from Popery, or in the whole range of evangelical piety—principles for which the Baptist denomination alone have consistently and unwaveringly contended during the last hundred years—principles now regarded with favor by evangelical Christians of other denominations, but in great danger of being weakened and disregarded. So long as infant baptism is preached, a Newman, or a Pusey, or a Nevin, or a Schaff, can, without much torturing, convert it into an acknowledgment of baptismal regeneration on the one side, and a Stoddard or a Bushnell make it the entering wedge of a lax church-membership on the other."*

* See the excellent work by Rev. Prof. Curtis of the University at Lewisburg, Pa., on The Progress of Baptist Principles in the Last Hundred Years, p. 73–85 (Chap. IV.)

VII.

INFANT BAPTISM AND INFANT CHURCH MEMBERSHIP.

WHEN the apostle Paul, in his epistle to Titus, mentions, among the qualifications that would indicate the suitableness of a man for the office of a bishop, his being "the husband of one wife," and his "having faithful children, not accused of riot or unruly," he probably did not intend to be understood as saying that no man could be a bishop who was not a husband, or who had not children, or whose children were not all believers; but rather that his being a husband worthily exemplifying marriage as it was at first divinely instituted, and his having children so judiciously brought up in the nurture and admonition of the Lord that some or all of them were already baptized believers, would be circumstances highly favorable to his being selected. We cannot, therefore, perceive the necessity of thinking with Dr. Bushnell, that the children here are called faithful or believers "in a presumptive or merely anticipatory way;" or that the Ephesian and Colossian children are included by the apostle among the faithful brethren of the two cities in the same way. The interpretation given of Eph. vi: 1, seems to us forced and unsatisfactory. On these words (Children, obey your parents in the Lord), our author remarks: "It is not, Children in the Lord, or, Children obey in the Lord your parents; but it is, Obey them who are parents in the Lord; as if their parentage itself, in the flesh, were a parentage also in the spirit, communicating both a personal and a Christian life. So also," he adds, "when the parents are required to give a nurture in the Lord, we may see that the children are expected to be grown as saints and faithfuls, and to be presumptively in the Lord, apart from any expectations and processes of adult conversion." We cannot help thinking that if he had no particular theory to maintain, he would himself be satisfied with the short and simple note on this passage, in the Tract Society's edition of the Bible: "*Obey your parents:* it is to be understood here, as in chap. v: 24, that the obedience enjoined extends to all things not contrary to Christ's commands; for the addition, *in the Lord,* that is, obey as those who are in the Lord, or make his will the law of their being, excludes obedience to those commands which are contrary to Christ's word."

Be this as it may, Dr. Bushnell proceeds thus: "And it was out of such uses that the term *faithful* grew into the peculiar kind of church use in which it denotes all the supposed members of the Christian body, whether adults or only baptized children. . . . The very language supposes a membership in the church, or among the faithful brethren, by virtue of baptism, and mere Christian nurture: such as on the footing of strict individualism, held by our Baptist brethren, could never even be thought of."

But has he proved that in the passages in Titus, Ephesians and Colossians, the very language supposes such a membership in the church, or among the faithful brethren, by virtue of infant baptism and mere Christian nurture, as on the footing of the individualism held by the Baptists, could never even be thought of? His comment and paraphrase are unsatisfactory; and we cannot admit that the language in those passages supposes what he infers and affirms.

The well-authenticated and simple fact is, that the term faithful grew into its peculiar kind of church use from the corresponding Latin and Greek words (fidelis and πιστὸς). In John xx: 27, our Saviour says to Thomas, "Be not incredulous, but believing."* Here in the Latin vulgate, *fidelis* is the translation of the Greek word (πιστὸς) corresponding to the English *believing* or *having faith*, faithful. So it is in Titus i: 6, having faithful children; Ephesians i: 1, to the faithful in Christ Jesus; and in Coloss. i: 2, to the saints and faithful brethren. Chrysostom, in one of his Homilies, explains the use of the Greek word: "Thou art called a faithful, a believer, because thou believest God."† In the earliest ages of Christianity,

---

* Noli esse incredulus, sed fidelis. *Μὴ γίνου ἄπιστος ἀλλὰ πιστός.*

† *Πιστὸς διὰ τοῦτο καλῇ, ὅτι πιστεύεις τῷ Θεῷ.* Hom. XXI. ad populum Antiochenum.

they who were baptized were baptized upon a profession of their faith. They were decided believers. "The faithful, the believers (όι πιστοί), is the name which has uniformly been used to denote such as have been duly instructed in the fundamental principles of the Christian religion, and have been received, by baptism, into the communion of the Church. By this name they were distinguished on the one hand from infidels and heretics, and on the other from the catechumens, etc.* Even since the introduction of infant baptism, the name has been retained by the baptized. "And so," as Augustine says in his sophistical letter to Boniface, "and so an infant, though he be not yet constituted a believer (fidelis) by that faith which consists in the will of believers, yet he is by the sacrament of that faith; for, as [in the preliminary part of the baptismal ceremony] he is said to believe, so he is called a believer."

After his expository introduction, Dr. Bushnell now proceeds to discuss *the church membership of baptized children.* He proposes to show the nature and kind of this membership; the reasons why it should exist; and the fact of its existence.

"The conception," he says, "of this membership is, that it is a potentially real one; that it stands, for the present, in the faith of the parents, and the promise

* See the Antiquities of the Christian Church, translated and compiled from the works of Augusti and others, by the Rev. Lyman Coleman, p. 58.

which is to them and to their children, and that on this ground they may well enough be accounted believers, just as they are accounted potentially men and women. Then, as they come forward into maturity, it is to be assumed that they will come for ward into faith, being grown in the nurture of faith, and will claim for themselves the membership into which they were before inserted." He finds a case analogous in the fact that our common law makes every infant a citizen. "What," he supposes it may be asked, "can the child do as a citizen? He cannot vote, nor bear arms; he does not even know what these things mean; and yet he is a citizen. In one view he votes, bears arms, legislates, even in his cradle; for the potentiality is in him, and the state takes him up in her arms, as it were, to own him as her citizen. In a strongly related sense, it is, that the baptized-child is a believer and a member of the church. There is no unreality in the position assigned him; for the futurition of God's promise is in him; and by a kind of sublime anticipation, he is accepted in God's supernatural economy as a believer, even as the law accepts him, in the economy of society, to be a citizen."

But why "the *baptized* child?" Does the sacrament of faith make the infant a believer, either instantly or prospectively? Why does the church, the ecclesiastical community, restrict her spiritual care and kindness and the blessings of the gospel to baptized children? The civil community, more god-like, extends care and kindness to all, without distinction. Where is Dr. Bushnell's authority for affirming that the futurition of God's promise is in the baptized child, any more than in one that has not been baptized, both being wisely brought up in the nurture and admonition of the Lord? Let the promise referred to be distinctly pointed out. In what chapter and verse of the Holy Scriptures is it to be found?

Among the reasons why infant membership should exist, or be appointed, the following are mentioned:

"First of all, if there is really no place in the Church of God for infant children, then it must be said, and formally maintained, that there is none. And what could be worse in its effect on a child's feeling, than to find himself repelled from the brotherhood of God's elect, in that manner? What can the hapless creature think either of himself or of God, when he is told that he is not old enough to be a Christian, or be owned by the Saviour as a disciple?"

We are happy in being able to assure Dr. Bushnell that we repel no child in this manner. We would welcome and encourage the little one's feeblest aspirations to become a loving and dutiful disciple of the Saviour. We would make a distinction, here overlooked, between the child that is a mere infant, and the child that is of sufficient maturity to participate, understandingly and with spiritual benefit, in the ordinances of Christianity, and to appreciate a union with the church.

"Again," he remarks, "it would be most remarkable, if Christianity, organizing a fold of grace and love in the world and for it, had yet no place in the fold for children. It spreads its arms to say: 'For God so loved the world,' and yet it has no place, we are told, for children; children are out of the category of grace! Jesus himself was a child, and went through all the phases and conditions of childhood. . . . He said, too, 'Suffer little children;' but this was only his human feeling; he had no official relationship to such, and no particular grace for them! They are all outside the salvation fold, hardening there in the storm, till their choosing, refusing, desiring, sinning power is sufficiently unfolded to have a place assigned them within! Is this Christianity? . . . In this view, it gives to little children the heritage only of Cain, requiring them to be driven out from the presence of the Lord, and grow up there among the outside crew of aliens and enemies. Let no one be surprised that, under such treatment, they stiffen into alienated, wrathful men, ripened for wickedness."

It is certainly surprising that Dr. Bushnell should think this to be a just representation of Christianity without the baptism and church membership of infants. Parental affection itself, united with wisdom, may deem the nursery a place more suitable for children than the lyceum or town-hall; and it may place them at a preparatory school, before it sends them to the university, or insists on their being admitted there.

In ancient times, persons won from heathenism, and children the offspring of Christian parents, were carefully instructed before they were baptized. Even so late as in the time of Augustine, according to his own testimony, as we have seen, it was a common thing to inquire respecting a Christian's child, Is he a catechumen, or a believer?. That is, Is he still receiving preparatory instruction, or has he been baptized as a believer? And Eusebius, in his Evangelic Demonstration, speaking in a general way, as one might speak of a people under a pastor's care or constituting a Christian congregation, says: There are three orders in each church or congregation; one, that of the leaders, and two, those of persons under them; the people of the Church of Christ being divided into two orders, into that of believers, and into that of the persons not yet esteemed worthy of the regeneration by the laver,* that is (more briefly), the people being divided into two orders, the decided believers, and the not yet baptized. These last, who were not yet deemed suitable for baptism, doubtless were, in various ways, receiving Christian nurture and instruction.

For such persons, according to the so-called Apostolic Constitutions, special prayer in their presence was offered, "that God would teach them

* Τρία καθ' ἑκάστην ἐκκλησίαν τάγματα, ἓν μὲν τὸ τῶν ἡγουμένων, δύο δὲ τὰ τῶν ὑποβεβηκότων, τοῦ τῆς ἐκκλησίας τοῦ Χριστοῦ λαοῦ εἰς δύο τάγματα διῃρημένου, εἴς τε τὸ τῶν πιστῶν, καὶ τῶν μηδέπω τῆς διὰ λουτροῦ παλιγγενεσίας ἠξιωμένων. Demonstrat. Evangel. Lib. vii., p. 200.

his commands and his ordinances, implant in them his saving and holy fear, open the ears of their hearts, strengthen them in piety, and *unite them to and number them with his flock*. . . . O God, who through thy Christ didst appoint the disciples to be teachers, that men might learn piety; do thou thyself even now look down upon thy servants who are catechised in the gospel of thy Christ, and give them *a new heart, and renew a right spirit in their inward parts*, that they may both know and do thy will with full purpose of heart, and with a willing soul. Account them worthy of the holy initiation, and unite them to thy holy church, and make them partakers of the holy mysteries, through Christ our hope, who for them suffered death; through whom glory and worship be given to thee in the Holy Spirit, forever. Amen "*

Here are persons not immediately admitted to baptism and church membership; and yet, who will say that they were harshly repelled? And is it right to insinuate that the Baptist principle, in regard to baptism and church membership "gives to little children the heritage only of Cain, requiring them to be driven out from the presence of the Lord, and grow up there among the outside crew of aliens and enemies?"

More than thirty years ago, the Baptist denomination in this country published, at Philadelphia, a tract entitled The Duty of giving Christian Instruc-

* Book viii. Chap. vi.

tion to Children.* "*This duty*," it states, "*is*, in the first place, *the dictate of reason and affection*. Reason requires that the ignorant be instructed—and the more important the knowledge, the stronger is the argument for its being communicated. And the greater our affection for the persons needing instruction the more intense is our desire to have them instructed. Who does not pronounce it suitable that children be taught those things which may be useful to them in the present life? and who that loves his children does not desire to have them taught? Now, we take it for granted, that the knowledge of the Christian religion is more valuable than the knowledge of any other subject; for it fills the mind with the brightest conceptions of purity and benevolence; and it is connected with what has the promise of the life that now is, and of that which is to come. It is, then, most manifestly, and most emphatically, the dictate of reason and affection, that Christian instruction be given to children. Besides, *this duty is clearly implied in the general direction to make the gospel known*. In the command of our Saviour, *Preach the gospel to every creature*, it is clear that he would have Christian instruction given to all who are capable of being instructed. The common sense of every man understands the direction as having reference to moral agents only, and to all moral

---

* Number 124 in the catalogue of the American Baptist Publication Society.

agents belonging to the human family. The gospel is to be preached to all; and we are to encourage its ministers to go forth and instruct the most distant nations. Surely, then, our own children are not to be neglected; but so soon as they can understand, they are to be taught the simple and affecting story of our redemption, the first principles of the oracles of God. But further, *the duty of giving Christian instruction to children is expressly enjoined.* The Sacred Scriptures exhibit this duty in the most direct and positive manner: 'Provoke not your children to wrath,' says an apostle, 'but bring them up in the nurture and admonition of the Lord.' *Nurture* is the more general term, indicating the education or training up of children, which, we know, comprehends instruction and example, rewards and punishments, and whatever may be necessary in this work. *Admonition*, as here used, directs our attention particularly to the mind of the child, as that with which we have especially to do; and we are here taught that this nurture and admonition, or instilling into the mind, must be conformable to the spirit and instructions of our Lord. So clear and prominent is the duty. It is the manifest dictate of reason and affection; it is implied in the general direction to make the gospel known; and it is expressly enjoined. It rests, therefore, on an immovable foundation, and we need no other."

Views like these, we think, indicate somethin better than "giving to little children the heritage only of Cain."

Dr. Bushnell asks, "Where is the encroachment when Christian parents baptize their child into the same discipleship with themselves, and set it in the school of Christ?" We reply, that to baptize a babe is to encroach on our Lord's prerogative. It is virtually to derange what he arranged, to annul what he ordained, to change what he appointed as an act of self-consecration, and profession of faith and obedience, into an act of consecrating another, and of promising that another believe and obey. In regard to the child, it is an encroachment on his right, when he becomes a disciple, of being consciously present, and participating in his own baptism, and of recalling it to mind afterwards, with spiritual benefit. Let the parents set their child in the school of Christ, according to their best ability and judgment; but who has authorized them to suppose that there is no place in that school for the little one, unless it be baptized?

Next, we are urged to consider "the remarkable and certainly painful fact that, in the view which excludes infant baptism and the discipleship of children, the conversion itself of a parent operates a kind of dissolution in the family state, than which nothing can be more unnatural. . . . God's effectual calling is no such unnatural grace; it will never call the parents away from the children, to be themselves included in the great family of salvation, and look out in their joy to see their children fenced away!"

Here again we have "infant baptism and the discipleship of children" placed together, as if they were inseparable companions, and one could not exist without the other. Why is this? It does not accord with the facts that have fallen under our observation. We never knew a parent who, in consequence of being converted and uniting with a Baptist church, became indifferent to the spiritual welfare of his children. We do not believe that such a case was ever known. And we are confident that the eloquence here expended on "the gathering of human parents away from their young," might have been more worthily employed.

Dr. Bushnell now inquires, "What will justify, or will naturally produce a more sullen remissness of duty in parents, than the fact that, for the present, God has shut away, and is holding away their children, and that they are never to be disciples of the fold, till after they have been passed round into it, through long detours of estrangement and ripening guiltiness? If there is nothing better for them than to be converted just as heathens are, why should they, as parents, be greatly concerned for their own example and the faithfulness of their training, when the conversion is to be every thing, and will have power to remedy every defect? How refreshing the contrast when the children, given to God in baptism, are accounted members of the Church with them, as being included in their faith, and having the seal of it upon them!"

Here infant baptism and infant church membership come as the grand remedy for tardiness of conversion among the children of Christians. Were there no better remedies than these, we should be overwhelmed with despondency. But we rejoice that without these, quite as well as with them, we may labor, and pray, and hope for early conversions. We may daily come to the Saviour, and in faith and love bring with us our children, to receive his blessing, to learn of him, and to imbibe his spirit. Train up a child in the way he should go, and when he is old, he will not depart from it.* In this, as in every duty, we acknowledge our dependence on God for success, and rejoice in the divine assurance that our heavenly Father is more disposed to "give the Holy Spirit to them that ask him," than we can be to give good gifts to our children.† Looking up to him as the gracious Being who works in us and in others "both to will and to do of his good pleasure,"‡ we hear the heavenly voice, "In the morning sow thy seed, and in the evening withhold not thine hand; for thou knowest not whether shall prosper, either this or that, or whether both shall be alike good."§ And then we have the apostle's exhortation and assurance, "Let us not be weary in well doing, for in due season we shall reap if we faint not."‖

Thus we have ample encouragement—all that is suitable, and possible in the nature of the case.

* Prov. xxii: 6. † Luke xi: 13.
‡ Phil. ii: 13. § Eccl. xi: 6.
‖ Gal. vi: 19.

Leaving out the baptism and church membership of infants, therefore, we have remaining a just and edifying description of truly Christian parents, when it is said, "Their prayers, they understand, are to keep heaven open upon their house. Their aims are to be Christian. Their tastes and manners are to be flavored by the Christian hope in which they live. There is to be a quickening element in the atmosphere they make. They will set all things upon a Christian footing for their children's sake; and their children, growing up in such nurture of the Lord, will, how certainly, unfold what their nurture itself has quickened."

Dr. Bushnell mentions as another consideration in favor of his system, that "the church itself, having this infant membership in it, will unfold other aims and tempers, and exert a finer quality of power. It will not be a dry convention of simply grown-up men and women. . . . The parents will learn from the children quite as much as they teach, and will do their teaching fitly, just because they learn. The Church prayers will have a certain paternity and maternity in them; and the children will feel the grace of these prayers warming always round them. . . . . And the whole volume of religious life will be unfolded by taking into itself the whole volume of nature and family feeling."

In the ancient church, as seen in the work claiming to be the Apostolical Constitutions, appropriate prayers were offered for the infants and for the catechumens, that they might be prepared for baptism and church membership. And we do not see why the children might not feel the grace of those prayers warming around them, and, in this respect, be as much benefited before as after their initiation. Besides, we fear that, in taking "the whole volume of nature and family feeling" into the church, more would be lost than gained by "the whole volume of religious life."

That the supposed infant membership is a real and true fact, Dr. Bushnell maintains "may be seen from the following proofs: 1. Those declarations of Scripture which assert or assume the fact. The Saviour commands, Suffer little children to come unto me, and forbid them not, for of such is the kingdom of heaven. . . . Nor," it is remarked, "is it any objection, as respects the children, that 'except a man be born again, he cannot be entered into this kingdom;' for, potentially at least, they are thus born again; and so are as fitly to be counted citizens of the kingdom, as they are to be citizens of the state. . . . And the great apostle to the Gentiles, in at least two of his epistles to Christian churches, addresses children, directly, as being included among the saints, and faithful in Christ Jesus."

2. The analogy of circumcision. "This," it is argued, "was given to be the seal of faith, and a church token, in that manner, of a godly seed. Baptism can certainly be the same with as little difficulty or as little charge of absurdity. True, they were not

all Israel that were of Israel; and so all may not be Israel that are baptized. Enough that God gives the possibility, in both cases, in giving the rite itself." But our readers will bear in mind that he *appointed* infant circumcision, not infant baptism; and that the design of circumcision was very different from the design of baptism as instituted by our Lord. Abraham received the sign of circumcision, a seal of the righteousness of the faith which he had yet being uncircumcised, that he might be the father of all them that believe.* In Jesus Christ neither circumcision availeth any thing, nor uncircumcision, but faith which worketh by love.† Baptism was designed to express the faith and devotedness of the baptized. If a person is bereft of reason, if through the violence of a fever, or of some accident, he becomes unconscious, is he to be baptized in his unconsciousness? If he is, on what ground, and by what authority? If he is not, then an unconscious infant is not to be baptized. Would not the administration of baptism in such a case, and in the case of an unconscious infant, be a manifest departure from the original design of baptism? Without a divine command, requiring it, we are unable to see how it could be justified.

In regard to children, Dr. Bushnell adds: "They must either be taken into the church, or else they must be excluded till they are old enough to be admitted

* Rom. iv: 11. † Gal. v: 6.

on the ground of a religious experience. There is no other alternative. If they are excluded, then it is taken for granted that they are to grow up as unbelievers and aliens, which is only their public consignment to evil." Taken for granted that they are to grow up as unbelievers and aliens! Not at all. The children are to be affectionately and carefully brought up by their parents in the nurture and admonition of the Lord; and their parents are to have the co-operation of the pastor, and the church, and the Sunday-school, and of all who would win the young to the Saviour and to the blessings here and hereafter, of becoming early his decided and faithful disciples.

The author proceeds: "If they are taken to be in the faith, presumptively, as in the nurture of their parents, and so accepted, then every kind encouragement is given to them, and every pledge of divine help is graciously given to their parents."

What pledge, we respectfully ask, what pledge of divine help is graciously given to the Pedobaptist parent that is withheld from the Baptist parent, on account merely of his conscientiously withholding baptism from his infant child?

We are next told that "God, on his part, gives no presumption, either to the parent or their child, that he is to be only a transgressor and alien; but he gives the seal of faith" (Does he?) "as a pledge, to raise their expectation of what he will do for them, and to throw the blame of a godless childhood and youth, if such there is to be, on themselves." Where, in all the Holy Scriptures, such a doctrine can be found, as the one here taught respecting the design of Christian baptism, we have been unable to discover.

3. The holiness of children, mentioned by the apostle Paul in 1 Cor. vii : 14, is urged as an argument for their church membership.

4. "All the reasons I have given," says Dr. Bushnell, "for the observance of infant baptism, go to establish also the fact of infant membership in the church. All this holds good, especially of that which discovers the origin of the rite in proselyte baptism."

Respecting the proofs under these two heads we do not deem it necessary here to make any remarks. We refer our readers to what we have already had occasion to present for their consideration.

Finally, in addition to the more direct evidences adduced for the church membership of baptized children, Dr. Bushnell urges "the opinions of the church and her most qualified teachers, from the apostolic era downward."

"This whole view of infant membership," he remarks, "as it stood in the first three centuries of the church history, appears to be well summed up, both as regards the facts and the reasons, in the following statement of Neander: 'It is the idea of infant baptism, that Christ, through the divine life which he imparted to, and revealed in, human nature, sanctified that germ from its earliest development. The child born in a Christian family was, when all things were as they should be, to have this advantage over others, that he did not come to Christianity out of heathenism or the sinful natural life, but from the first dawning of consciousness unfolded his powers under the imperceptible, preventing influences of a sanctifying, ennobling religion; that, with the earliest germinations of the natural self-conscious life, another divine principle of life, transforming the nature, should be brought nigh to him, ere yet the ungodly principle could come into full activity, and the latter should, at once, find here its powerful counterpoise. In such a life, the new birth was not to constitute a new crisis beginning at some definable moment, but it was to begin imperceptibly, and so proceed through the whole life. Hence baptism, the visible sign of regeneration, was to be given to the child at the very outset: the child was to be consecrated to the Redeemer from the very beginning of its life."*

This remarkable paragraph was occasioned by the passage in which Irenæus speaks of all as being regenerated to God through Christ. That the impartial and venerable historian should seem to acquiesce in the common erroneous opinion of its having reference to baptism, may easily have arisen from the intensity with which while, he was reading

* Neander's Church History (Torrey's translation), Vol. I., pp. 311, 312.

Irenæus, his mind was attracted to other matters than the one embraced in that passage. "Regeneration and baptism," he says, "are in Irenæus intimately connected; and it is difficult to conceive how the term regeneration can be employed in reference to this age [infancy], to denote any thing else than baptism. Infant baptism, then, appears here as the medium through which the principle of sanctification, imparted by Christ to human nature from its earliest development, became appropriated to children." How much does this fall short of baptismal regeneration? He now takes up "the profound Christian idea" which he supposes to have been in the mind of Irenæus, and from it, in conjunction with evangelical, and perhaps with some mixed ideas in his own mind, he skillfully develops a plausible theory of infant baptism—an apology for a practice, which, according to his own testimony, was not introduced till long after the time of the apostles.

Here begins Dr. Bushnell's quotation. Let us look at it again: "It is the idea of infant baptism, that Christ, through the divine life which he imparted to human nature, sanctified that germ from its earliest development. The child born in a Christian family was . . to be under the imperceptible, preventing influences of a sanctifying, ennobling religion. . . . A divine principle of life, transforming the nature, was to be brought nigh to him" (In baptism? or in Christian nurture? or in both?) "ere yet the ungodly principle could come into full activity. . . . The new birth was not to constitute a new crisis."

Obviously, however, the new birth must in reality be something new, though it begin, not at a definable moment, but imperceptibly, and so proceed through the whole life. When it became perceptible, and there was reasonable evidence of its existence, it would be proper and truthful to let it be indicated by an appropriate sign. "Hence" (on account of the imperceptibility of the beginning of the new birth) "baptism, the visible sign of regeneration, was to be given to the child at the very outset," says Neander, the accommodating theorist. When?! *When the child gave evidence of being spiritually regenerated*, says Neander, the conscientious historian. On the very same page on which the quoted paragraph begins, the historian states most explicitly, "*We have all reason for not deriving infant baptism from apostolic institution.*"

Shall we regard the historian, or the theorist? Shall we follow the Holy Scriptures, or the unauthorized devices of men?

To strengthen his argument, Dr. Bushnell next presents a statement from Cave's Primitive Christianity, illustrating the power of religion, as seen in the domestic life of families: "Gregory Nazianzen peculiarly commends his mother, that not only she herself was consecrated to God, and brought up under a pious education, but that she conveyed it down, as a necessary inheritance to her children, and it seems her daughter Gorgonia was so well seasoned with these holy principles, that she religiously walked in the steps of so good a pattern; and not only reclaimed her husband, but educated her children and nephews in the ways of religion."*

What renders this statement peculiarly instructive and valuable is, that the remarkably pious and exemplary parents of Gregory Nazianzen did not think it their duty to have their offspring baptized in infancy. It is well known that he did not receive baptism till he came to years of discretion; and yet at the time of his birth his father was a minister of the gospel.

Calvin is introduced, making the adventurous assertions that "children are baptized into future repentance and faith; for, though these graces have not yet been formed in them, the seeds of both are nevertheless implanted in their hearts by the secret operations of the Spirit." And Baxter is brought forward teaching the doctrine of infant baptism thus: "As children are made sinners and miserable by the parents, without any act of their own, so they are delivered out of it by the free grace of Christ, upon a condition performed by their parents."

In 1649, the Cambridge Platform limited church-membership to such as appeared to be renewed persons; while, throughout New England, except the Hartford and Providence colonies, none who were not members of the church were permitted to be

* Primitive Christianity, pp. 173-174.

voters in civil affairs. In 1662, all baptized persons who lived reputably and assented to the gospel, were allowed to be so far church members as to be voters in the commonwealth, and to have their children baptized.

We pass over Cotton Mather's unfavorable opinion in regard to "the way of the Anabaptists," and his favorable opinion in regard to "keeping persons under those church dispensations wherein grace is given."

Religion declined. After a long period in which the churches fell into a state of debility, and "well nigh lost the idea of spiritual life," there came the Great Revival, in 1740 and subsequent years, under the ministration of Whitefield, Edwards and others. This, in the circumstances of the people, was very naturally attended with some ill-regulated excitements and some defective or erroneous views. Speaking of the kind of religion favored and promoted by the friends of the revival, Dr. Bushnell says: "It has one great merit, and one great defect. The merit is that it displaced an era of dead formality, and brought the demand of a truly supernatural experience. The defect is, that it has cast a type of religious individualism, intense beyond any former example. It makes nothing of the family, and the church, and the organic powers God has constituted as vehicles of grace."

In this connection, and on this topic generally, we think that Dr. Bushnell's censure is so severe and indiscriminating as, in many cases, to become unjust.

His description is a caricature. It cannot have reference to Baptists alone. Doubtless, it was designed quite as much for some others, as for them, and it may be beneficial to all.

A pupil of Edwards, Dr. Hopkins, in his system of Divinity, discusses largely the nature and design of infant baptism. And he is now introduced. "He goes even beyond the notion of a presumptive piety in the children baptized, and says, 'The church receive and look upon them as holy, and those who shall be saved. So they are as visibly holy, or as really holy, in their view, as their parents are.' He asserts an organic connection of character between parents and children, as effectual for good as for evil; nay, that they may as truly, and in the same sense, transmit holiness as they transmit *existence;* not, indeed, independently of God, but by virtue of a covenant divinely constituted. 'If God,' it is affirmed, 'has been pleased to make a constitution and appoint a way in the covenant of grace with man, by which pious parents may convey and communicate moral rectitude or holiness to their children, they, by using the appointed means, do it as really and effectually as they communicate existence to them. In this sense, therefore, they may convey and give holiness and salvation to their children.'" On another page, Dr. Hopkins says: "Real holiness and salvation are secured to the children of believers, by the covenant into which the parents enter with God, as it respects their children, *when they offer them in baptism.*"* And "Jesus Christ does, in this transaction, receive the child into the same visible standing and character with the parent, as a visible saint, or holy person, and orders the church to consider and look upon it in this light."†

This assertion, that our Lord takes part in the transaction when an infant is baptized, assumes that infant baptism is one of his institutes. But we are constrained to believe that it was not instituted by him; and that it has no support, either in the Holy Scriptures or in the earliest ecclesiastical history. Its non-existence in the time of the apostles would prove the non-existence of infant church membership at that time; but baptism would naturally imply membership. And now, respecting the matter before us, what is the testimony of the most reliable works on Christian Antiquities? We refer our readers to the volume prepared by Professor Coleman. It can easily be procured. There (chap. xiv. sec. 3) they will find the following statement: "The general introduction of the rite of infant baptism has so far changed the regulations of the church concerning the qualifications of candidates, and their admission, that what was formerly the rule in this respect, has become the exception. The institutions of the church during the first five centuries, concerning the requisite preparations for baptism, and all the laws and rules that existed

* Vol. II., p. 291. † Vol. II., p. 286.

during that period, relating to the acceptance or rejection of candidates, necessarily fell into disuse when the baptism of infants began not only to be permitted, but enjoined as a duty; and almost universally observed. The old rule, which prescribed caution in the admission of candidates, and a careful preparation for the rite, was, after the sixth century, applicable, for the most part, only to Jewish, heathen and other proselytes. The discipline which was formerly requisite preparatory to baptism, now followed this rite."

The statement here made is corroborated by Bunsen, a writer distinguished alike for his frankness and for his extraordinary erudition. In his work on Hippolytus and his Age (about the beginning of the third century), he says: "The Apostolic Church made the school the connecting link between herself and the world. The object of this education was admission into the free society and brotherhood of the Christian community. The church adhered rigidly to the principle, as constituting the true purport of the baptism ordained by Christ, that no one can be a member of the communion of saints, but by his own free act and deed, his own solemn vow made in presence of the church. It was with this understanding that the candidate for baptism was immersed in water, and admitted as a brother, upon his confession of the Father, the Son and the Holy Ghost. It understood baptism, therefore, in the exact sense of the First Epistle of St. Peter (iii: 21), not as being a mere bodily purification, but as a vow made to God with a good conscience, through faith in Jesus Christ. Justin Martyr calls baptism a dedication of ourselves to God. This vow was preceded by a confession of Christian faith, made in the face of the church, in which the catechumen expressed that faith in Christ, and in the sufficiency of the salvation offered by him. It was a vow to live, for the time to come, to God and for his neighbor, not to the world and for self; a vow of faith in his becoming a child of God through the communion with his only begotten Son in the Holy Ghost; a vow of the most solemn kind, for life and for death. The keeping of this pledge was the condition of continuance in the church; its infringement entailed repentance or excommunication. All church discipline was based upon this voluntary pledge, and the responsibility thereby self-imposed. But how could such a vow be received without examination? How could such examination be passed without instruction and observation?

"As a general rule, the ancient church fixed three years for this preparation, supposing the candidate, whether heathen or Jew, to be competent to receive it. With Christian children the condition was the same, except that the term of probation was curtailed according to circumstances. Pedobaptism, in the more modern sense, meaning thereby baptism of new-born infants, with the vicarious promises of parents or other sponsors, was utterly unknown to the early church; not only down to the end of the second but indeed to the middle of the third century. We shall show, in a subsequent page, how, towards the close of the second century, this practice originated in the baptism of children of a more advanced age.

"Hence we find in the Christian school of that period, four great acts, three of which were common both to the new converts and to Christian children: previous examination of the Jewish or heathen candidates who presented themselves; instruction; examination immediately before immersion and the taking of the vow; and, lastly, that ceremony itself."*

Again we request our readers to ponder the considerations which have been presented. Are they not sufficient to show the groundlessness of Dr. Bushnell's arguments for infant baptism? Are they not sufficient to show that it was not instituted either by our Lord or by his apostles? And if it was not divinely instituted and sanctioned, it is an unauthorized human device, a perversion, an intrusion, crowding out (however unintentionally) what our Lord and Saviour did institute. Has it not a natural and strong tendency to open the way for untimely and unsuitable membership and unchristian character in the church, and for other departures from the regulations established by the wise and gracious Founder of Christianity? Ought it not then to be discontinued?

Notwithstanding Dr. Bushnell's sincere and earnest

---

* Vol. II. p. 105, 2d Ed.

rejection of the doctrine of Baptismal Regeneration, as held under the priestly forms of Christianity, some of the consequences of that doctrine must, almost inevitably, adhere to his system. Infant baptism arose at first, in great measure, from that doctrine; and while it exists, there will be imminent danger of its cherishing an undue and dangerous reliance on a ceremony. While it exists, disguise and adorn it as we may, it is still an unauthorized intrusion; and the more we disguise and adorn it, the more are evil consequences to be dreaded. The honor of our Lord and the interests of religion, throughout Christendom, require that infant baptism be discontinued. He, and he only, has a right to be obeyed in this matter. And for the churches and for all the individuals concerned, there is safety only in obedience to his rightful authority.

Let baptism, as it was instituted by him, be restored. The way is open for Christian nurture in all its amplitude and all its blessedness. The parent's duty is made as clear and imperative as the most intelligible words can express a command. The parent is directly responsible; and, at the same time, he is to seek and receive all needed help. It is an error, if any suppose that we welcome only late or explosive conversions. We would gladly accept the child, with the child's experience. We ask only for reasonable evidence that he cordially loves the Saviour, and humbly relying on his grace, desires, with deliberate purpose, to serve and honor him forever.

The American Baptist Publication Society, in the Tract which has already been mentioned as having been issued many years ago, gives the following representation: "That, in the time of our Lord there were children who had received the truth in the love of it, is evident from the twenty-first chapter of Matthew, where it is stated: 'When the chief priests and scribes saw the wonderful things that he did, and the children crying in the temple, and saying Hosanna to the Son of David, they were displeased, and said unto him, Hearest thou what these say? And Jesus saith unto them, Yea; have ye never read, Out of the mouths of babes and sucklings thou hast perfected praise?' This is a quotation from the eighth Psalm; and, it being poetry, it is somewhat hyperbolical, according to the poetic manner, but the idea intended to be exhibited is perfectly manifest, namely, that God is pleased when young children feel his love, and utter his praise.

"Instances of early piety have occurred in almost every age of the world; and they are not rare in our own country at the present time. Within the circle of our own observation, and particularly in those places where special attention has been paid to the subject of religion, many a striking and lovely example of this kind has presented itself; and we have been most happily taught the force of the passage, *Out of the mouths of babes and sucklings, thou hast perfected praise.* Indeed, there is abundant proof that genuine conversions may occur, and that they have occurred, at a very early period. Why, then, we ask again, why should we not hope, and labor and pray for such a blessing in respect to our own children ?"

Expressions like these ought to have protected our denomination from Dr. Bushnell's unfavorable representations. It is not our Christian principles, but our failing to live up to them, that is to be censured. In our endeavors we will welcome help, from whatever quarter it may come, and in whatever form, whether of reproach or of commendation, of encouragement or of admonition. *Let the righteous smite me: it shall be a kindness; and let him reprove me: it shall be an excellent oil.**

The volume before us contains much that is valuable. Besides the discourses or essays in which the arguments occur which we have been reviewing, there are eight or ten others. One of them is on "the ostrich nurture;" one on "the out-populating power of the Christian stock;" and another is entitled, "when and where the nurture begins." The rest are on parental qualifications; physical nurture to be a means of grace; the treatment that discourages piety; family government; plays and pastimes; holidays and Sundays; the Christian teaching of children; and family prayer. Without approving every sentiment expressed, we commend the perusal of the book to

* Psalms cxli: 5

the discriminating reader. He will find it highly interesting and suggestive.

Would that the author might have health and a disposition to prepare an improved edition, thoroughly expurgated of the present errors, and thus furnish, on a subject of immense importance, a volume that might be a worthy companion for his recently published sermons, and for his thrice welcome chapter on the character of Christ.

THE TESTIMONY OF ORIGEN.

THE TESTIMONY OF ORIGEN

RESPECTING THE BAPTISM OF CHILDREN.

ORIGEN, it will be recollected, was born at Alexandria, in the year of our Lord 185, and died at Tyre, in the year 254. Like many of the early fathers—for example, like Clement, his learned and ingenious predecessor in the catechetical school, at Alexandria—he conceived of Christian baptism as having a miraculous, renewing efficacy on those who were already converted, penitent and believing, or, as we should say, already renewed.

The following remarkable passage occurs in his commentary on John: "Moreover, it is fitting to know that as the wonderful powers in the cures wrought by the Saviour, being symbols of the persons who perpetually are liberated by the word of God from every disease and malady of the soul, were none the less beneficial, though exerted on the body, inasmuch as they called to faith those who were benefited; so the laver by the water, being a symbol of the purification of the soul, washed in regard to all pollution from iniquity, is, to him who presents himself to the Deity, none the less and OF ITSELF *the* *source and fountain of divine gifts*, on account of the power of the invocations of the adorable Trinity."*

Here is a prolific error. Reliance on the wonderful efficacy in itself, at first figuratively, and then unduly ascribed to the administration of baptism, soon and easily, in conjunction with other causes, led the way to a partial overlooking of the qualifications formerly required of every individual that was to be baptized. But Origen did not overlook them. In his work against Celsus, as well as in the passage just now cited, he calls baptism "The symbol of having been purified."†

In his Commentary on John, he speaks of baptism, indeed, as being "performed in connection with the renewing of the Spirit, which," he adds, "as it is from God, even now moves upon the water; but," he acknowledges, "it is not in all the baptized."‡

Hence he often urges the catechumens (as in Homily VI. 5, on Ezekiel, and Homily XXI. on Luke)

---

* Χρὴ δὲ εἰδέναι ὅτι ὥσπερ αἱ κατὰ τὰς γεγενημένας ὑπὸ τοῦ σωτῆρος θεραπείας τεράστιοι δυνάμεις, σύμβολα τυγχάνουσαι τῶν ἀεὶ λόγῳ τοῦ θεοῦ ἀπαλλαττομένων πάσης νοσου καὶ μαλακίας, οὐδὲν ἧττον καὶ σωματικῶς γενομέναι ὤνησαν, εἰς πίστιν προσκαλεσάμεναι τοὺς εὐεργετηθέντας· οὕτως καὶ τὸ διὰ τοῦ ὕδατος λουτρὸν, σύμβολον τυγχάνον καθαρσίου ψυχῆς, πάντα ῥύπον ἀπὸ κακίας ἀποπλυνομένης, οὐδὲν ἧττον καὶ κατ' αὐτὸ τῷ ἐμπαρέχοντι ἑαυτὸν τῇ θειότητι τῆς δυνάμεως τῶν τῆς προσκυνητῆς τριάδος ἐπικλήσεων, ἔστιν ἡ χαρισμάτων θείων ἀρχὴ καὶ πηγή. Tom. vi., 17.

† Τὸ σύμβολον τοῦ ἀποκεκαθάρθαι. B. iii., 51.

‡ . . . . μετὰ ἀνακαινώσεως γινόμενον πνεύματος, τοῦ καὶ νῦν ἐπιφερομένου, ἐπειδὴ παρὰ θεοῦ ἐστιν, ἐπάνω τοῦ ὕδατος, ἀλλ' οὐ πᾶσι μετὰ τὸ ὕδωρ ἐγγινομένου. Tom. vi., 17.

to make a worthy preparation, and come to baptism in a suitable state of mind, so that they may be washed into salvation.* Speaking in regard to baptism in Homily XXVI. on Luke, he says, "If thou be holy, thou shalt be baptized in the Holy Spirit."† And, in the same connection, he further says, "To these who are holy and with entire faith are converted to the Lord there will be given, in baptism, the grace of the Holy Spirit and salvation."‡

In his Homily III. 1, on Numbers, he remarks, "Not all that are of Israel are Israelites. Nor does it follow as a matter of course that all who have been washed in the water have also been washed in the Holy Spirit; and, on the other hand, not all are aliens and destitute of the Holy Spirit who are numbered among the catechumens.§

From the record in Luke 4 : 20, that the eyes of all that were in the synagogue were fastened on our Lord, Origen, in his thirty-second Homily on that book, takes occasion to exclaim, "Happy the congregation concerning which the Scripture testifies that the eyes of all were attentive to him! How I could

---

* Ut veniatis ad lavacrum, et lavemini in salutem.

† Si sanctus fueris, Spiritu Sancto baptizaberis.

‡ His vero qui sancti sunt, et tota fide ad Dom.num convertuntur, Spiritus Sancti gratia salusque tribuenda est.

§ Non enim omnes qui ex Israel,ii sunt Israelitæ: Neque omnes qui loti sunt aqua, continuo etiam Sancto Spiritu loti sunt; sicut e contrario non omnes qui in catechumenis numerantur, alieni sunt et expertes Spiritus Sancti.

wish this assembly to have similar testimony, that the eyes of all, of catechumens and believers, of women and men and infants, the eyes not of the body but of the soul, were attentively beholding Jesus!"*

As we proceed, let it not be forgotten that Origen here uses the word *infants* (infantes, νήπιοι) to indicate the children of his congregation; children, the eyes of whose minds might attentively behold the Saviour.

Decisive evidence in support of Infant Baptism, it has been thought by many, is to be found in the works of Origen. Three passages have been brought forward and urged with much confidence: one from his Homilies on Leviticus; another from his Homilies on Luke; and the third from his Commentary on the Epistle to the Romans.

From a very early period, these passages have had great influence. And their influence has been much increased by their being ingeniously set forth in Mr. Wall's History of Infant Baptism, first published in England, about a hundred and fifty years ago. The cause of truth seems to demand that they be carefully and candidly examined. In view of the present state of Christendom, we think it important

* Beata congregatio de qua Scriptura testatur, quod omnium oculi erant attendentes in eum! Quam vellem istum cœtum simile habere testimonium, ut omnium oculi, et catechumenorum, et fidelium, et mulierum, et virorum, et infantium, non corporis oculi, sed animæ, aspicerent Jesum!

that they be rightly appreciated. We would invite attention to the subject, and submit to all candid inquirers some considerations which, we hope, will assist them in coming to a just and satisfactory conclusion.

Before introducing the passages themselves, it ought to be recollected that they exist, not in the Greek language, in which they were written by Origen, but only in the Latin, into which they were translated near the close of the fourth century. The Homilies on Luke were translated by Jerome; those on Leviticus and the Commentary on the Epistle to the Romans, by Rufin.

On general principles, it must be admitted that a translation is not so reliable an authority as the original; and in the cases before us, there are some special considerations that are adapted to awaken our distrust.

It is well known that the works of Origen have suffered greatly, not only from the unintentional injuries of time, but also from injuries more deplorable. Some of them, from various motives, have been curtailed; and some have been interpolated. Many have suffered both by omissions and by additions. Many, too, whose originals no longer exist, were more or less deformed by the translator, when they were transferred from the Greek language into the Latin.

In regard to Jerome, few need to be informed that he took great liberties in translating works of Origen.

He did, indeed, reproach Rufin for making certain unwarrantable changes. But the circumstances were peculiar.

Jerome and Rufin had been early and intimate friends. Their studies, their habits of mind, and their manner of living, in Italy and in Palestine, had, in many respects, been similar. Both were zealous churchmen. Both were monks: and both were presbyters. Both were highly distinguished for enterprise, for untiring diligence, and for extensive learning, especially in ecclesiastical literature. Jerome was pre-eminent for his knowledge of Hebrew, and for translating the Holy Scriptures. Rufin, in bringing out his translation of that speculative and adventurous work of Origen, entitled, *On first Principles*,* was desirous, it is probable, of commending it to the favorable regard of its readers through the influence of Jerome, who had translated other works of the same author. In his preface he referred to him respectfully as a brother and colleague, whose example and manner of translating he had endeavored to follow; and he used such other expressions as, in connection with these, made Jerome apprehensive of being himself suspected of Origenism, which was then regarded by many as a most dangerous heresy.† Jerome was

* Περὶ ἀρχῶν.

† Frater et collega in præfatiuncula vocor, et satis apertè exponuntur crimina mea, quid scripserim, quibus in cœlum Origenem laudibus levaverim. . . . Voluerat me in interpretatione quasi prævium sequi; et auctoritatem operi suo ex nostris opusculis mutuari. See in Jerome's Works, vol. iv., p. 349, his *Apologia adversus Rufinum*, lib. 1.

indignant. He doubtless suspected Rufin of being at once heretical and disingenuous. He resolved to clear himself, and overwhelm a popular rival.

In his defense or apology against Rufin, he represented him as having changed for the better, the doctrines which Origen had taught, concerning the Father, and the Son, and the Holy Spirit, and which Roman ears were unable to bear, while he had retained others equally heretical, and had sometimes added confirmations to them ; *so that he who should read what was sound on the Trinity, would not avoid what was unsound on other subjects.** The orthodoxy on one point of great interest would allure and encourage men to receive what was heretical on many others.

Thus Rufin, in the view of Jerome, had been laboring to promote pernicious errors. This was "the head and front of his offending." It was not so much

---

* Quæ quum legissem, contulissemque cum Græco, illico animadverti quæ Origenes de Patre et Filio et Spiritu Sancto impiè dixerat ; et quæ Romanæ aures ferre non poterant, in meliorem partem ab interprete commutata. Cætera autem dogmata, de angelorum ruina, de animorum lapsu ; de resurrectionis præstigiis ; de mundo vel intermundiis Epicuri ; de restitutione omnium in æqualem statum ; et multa his deteriora, quæ longum esset retexere, vel ita vertisse, ut in Græco invenerat ; vel de commentariolis Didymi, qui Origenis apertissimus propugnator est, exaggerata et firmiora posuisse *ut qui in Trinitate Catholicum legeret, in aliis Hæreticum non caveret.* *Apol. adversus Ruf.*, lib. i., (vol. iv., p. 355.)

that he had changed certain passages, as that in doing this and in writing his preface, he had been artfully preparing the way for the reception of doctrines contrary to those of the church. Jerome says in reference to his own effort in exhibiting the true version, " I have dragged forth and given up the Heretic, that I might vindicate the Church from heresy."*

A long and bitter controversy ensued, relative mainly to speculative opinions and to personal matters, about which we rejoice that we have no necessity here to speak.

In regard to the changes, Rufin replies that he had followed the example of Jerome; and he brings two instances, one from the Homilies on Luke, and the other from those on Isaiah, where, in passages connected with the doctrine of the Trinity, Jerome departs from the Greek original of Origen, and inserts something of his own, intended to present a better view.† In the same connection he says to Jerome: " To translate, word for word, thou hast heretofore pronounced to be stupid and malicious. In this I have followed thee. Of this dost thou wish me to repent, because thou hast lately changed thine opinion, and sayest that thou translatest word for word? If respecting the faith there occur things that are unedi-

* Prodidi Hæreticum, ut Ecclesiam ab hæresi vindicarem. *Ib.*, p. 357.

† See the second book of Rufin's "*Invectives*," inserted among the works of Jerome (Benedictine edition, Paris, 1706), vol. iv., p. 438.

fying, thou hast omitted them; and yet not so as to cut them away entirely and in all places. . . . . I, too, have done the same very frequently, and have either omitted some expressions, or given them such a turn as to present a sense more beneficial. For these acts dost thou think that I ought to repent? I do not believe that thou thinkest so."*

From what has already been stated it appears that Jerome, since he had no heretical design, thought it right in himself to omit or alter what was erroneous in the writings of Origen, and to insert freely, at his own discretion, what in his view was correct and in harmony with the spirit of the original. We need not cite what he himself, in various places, acknowledges and defends, and claims credit for doing; as in his epistle (xxxix. aliàs 62) to Alexander; where, in reply to an accusation against him that he had translated Origen, he says, "This not only I have done, but also the confessor Hilary; and yet each of us, omitting whatever things were noxious, translated

* Verbum de verbo interpretari: antea, et stultum esse et malitiosum, pronunciasti. In hoc secutus sum te. Nunquid de hoc vis ut pœniteat me, quia tu modo mutasti sententiam, et ad verbum interpretatum te dicis? Si qua in fide minus ædificabant, abstulisti: ut non omnia nec in omnibus penitus amputares. . . . . . Hæc et ego in quamplurimis feci, et aut desecavi aut ad saniorem intelligentiam declinavi. Pro his me jubes agere pœnitentiam? Non puto hoc te sentire.

the useful."* We need not cite the assertions of learned men. Let it suffice just to mention one whom all will admit to be a competent and unprejudiced judge. We allude to De La Rue, the editor of the Benedictine edition of the works of Origen. In his preface to the third volume, he adverts to the conjecture of Daillè that the Homilies on Luke were not written in Greek and so early as the time of Origen, since they contain indications of a later age; and he remarks that the appearances alluded to might be accounted for, in part, by recollecting that the translator was *Jerome; whose usual manner in translating Greek,* he adds, *the learned know to have been, to insert occasionally some things of his own.*†

Nor need we bring examples from his translation of Eusebius's Chronicon, or from any other works of Origen, than these Homilies on Luke that are now before us. In these there are omissions, and there are additions. Certain things to which Origen refers in his Commentary on Matthew and on John,‡ as having been discussed in his Homilies on Luke, have been omitted; and there are other evidences that the work has been abridged. But of this there is no intimation on the part of Jerome. In his preface, he

* Hoc non solus ego feci; sed et confessor Hilarius fecit: et tamen uterque nostrum noxia quæque detruncans, utilia transtulit.

† Hieronum: cui in vertendis Græcis sciunt eruditi solemne esse nonnulla interdum de suo inserere.

‡ On Matthew, tom. xiii., 29 and on John, tom. xxxii., 2.

speaks of translating the Homilies as they are in the Greek. At the same time, he leads us to expect that he would hold in contempt nice and exact conformities to *words* and *sentences.** He therefore confirms the statement of Rufin on this point. There are also, it is certain, some additions. One of considerable extent may be found in the thirtieth Homily.

Fragmentary parts of the Greek original of the Homilies on Luke have been brought to light. They were gathered from various manuscripts in England and in France, by the diligent researches of the eminent scholars whose names they bear. They are known as the Fragments of Grabe and Combefis;† and they are inserted as notes at the bottom of the page in the Benedictine edition of Origen. Few and short as they are, they enable us, as far as they extend, to compare the translation with the original. In this way, independently of all other evidence, we ascertain that in these very Homilies on Luke, Jerome added freely as well as omitted.

---

*Jerome's preface to his translation of Origen's Homilies on Luke is addressed to his munificent female friends, Paula and Eustochium. It begins thus: Ante paucos dies quorundam in Matthæum et Lucam Commentarios vos legisse dicistis: è quibus alter et sensibus hebes esset: et alter in *verbis* luderet, in *sententiis* dormitaret. Quamobrem petitis, ut *istiusmodi nugis contemptis*, saltem triginta et novem Adamantii nostri in Lucam Homilias, sicut in Græco habentur, interpreter.

† Schedæ Grabii et Combefisii.

The addition which we have mentioned as being in the thirtieth Homily is longer than the passage quoted from the fourteenth in favor of infant baptism. It is inserted in the midst of what is now the Greek Fragment; and it furnishes an admirable illustration of the freedom with which, from his preface and from other sources, we might suppose that he would translate works of Origen. Like that passage, it is supplementary; and it falls in with the drift of the preceding discourse, but has no necessary connection with it. For the entire satisfaction of every reader, we place in a note the Greek of Origen and the Latin of Jerome, with a plain English version of both.*

---

* The subject of remark is the second temptation of our Lord, as recorded in Luke 4: 5–8.

A GREEK FRAGMENT OF ORIGEN'S HOMILY XXX. ON LUKE.

ἔδειξεν αὐτῷ πάσας τὰς βασιλείας τῆς οἰκουμένης. βασιλείας κόσμου φησὶ τῶν κοσμικῶν ἀνθρώπων, τίνα τρόπον οἱ μὲν βασιλεύονται ὑπὸ φιλαργυρίας, οἱ δὲ ὑπὸ κενοδοξίας. εἰ μὴ γὰρ τοῦτό ἐστι, πῶς ἠδύνατο ἀυτὸυς τόπους ἐις ἕνα τόπον πρὸς θεωρίαν σωματικὴν ἀγαγεῖν, οἷον, φέρε ἐιπεῖν, τὴν Περσῶν ἡγεμονίαν, ἢ τὴν Ἰνδῶν; καὶ γὰρ ἐδείκνυον αὐτῷ τὰς βασιλείας τοῦ κόσμου τίνα τρόπον ἰσχύει βασιλεύειν, ἵνα ἀὐτὸν προτρέψηται ποιῆσαι ὃ ἐνόμιζε ποιῆσαι περιγενήσεσθαι τοῦ σωτῆρος. εἰ θέλεις, φησὶ, βασιλεῦσαι τούτων, καὶ ἐπὶ τοῦτο ἐλήλυθας τοῦ ἀγωνίσασθαι, καὶ ἀποστῆσαι τοὺς βασιλευομένους ὑπ' ἐμοὶ, μὴ ἀγωνίζου· ἓν ἀξιῶ, πεσὼν προσκυνησόν μοι, καὶ παράλαβε πᾶσαν τὴν βασιλείαν τὴν ὑπ' ἐμέ. ἀλλ' ὁ σωτὴρ βασιλέυσαι μὲν θέλει καὶ ὑποτάξαι πάντα τὰ ἔθνη, ἵνα δοῦλα γένηται τῆς δικαιοσύνης καὶ ἀληθείας καὶ πάσης ἀρετῆς. βασιλεῦσαι δὲ οὐ μετὰ ἁμαρτίας, οὐδὲ βόυλεται ἀκμητὶ ὑποτάξας αὐτὸν ἐκείνῳ ἐστεφανῶσθαι, οὐδὲ ἀκμητὶ λαβεῖν πάσας τὰς βασιλέιας τοῦ κόσμου καὶ τὴν δόξαν αὐτῶν ὑποχέιριον, διὰ φησι πρὸς αὐτον, γέγραπται, κύριον τὸν θεόν σου προσκυνήσεις, καὶ αὐτῷ μόνῳ λατρέυσεις.

Now if Jerome has made such an addition in the thirtieth Homily; if he has freely omitted or added more or less elsewhere; if he was accustomed to do this, in accordance with what he believed to be true

---

(The tempter) *showed to him all the kingdoms of the world.* Kingdoms of the world, he says of worldly men—how some are governed by avarice, and some by vain-glory. For unless this be the meaning, how was it possible to bring into one place the places themselves for a bodily view, as, for example, the kingdom of the Persians, or that of the Indians? He showed him therefore how he is able to reign over the kingdoms of the world, that he might incite him to do what he thought would accomplish his overcoming the Saviour. If thou desirest, he saith, to reign over these; and for this thou hast come forth, to have a contest, and to lead into a revolt those who are governed by me—do not contend. One thing I request: falling down worship me; and receive the whole kingdom that is under me. But the Saviour wishes indeed to reign, and to subject all the nations, that they may be servants of righteousness and of truth and of every virtue; but to reign without sin. Nor does he wish to be crowned without labor, subjecting himself to that [evil] one; nor without labor to receive all the kingdoms of the world and their subjected glory. Wherefore he saith to him, It is written *Thou shalt worship the Lord thy God, and him only shalt thou serve.*

THE LATIN TRANSLATION, AS PRESENTED BY JEROME.

Ostendit ei omnia regna mundi, et hominum hujus sæculi, quomodo alii regnentur à fornicatione, alii ab avaritia, illi populari rapiantur aura, hi formæ capiantur illecebris. Neque verò arbitrandum est, quod regna ei mundi ostendens,

and orthodox, and for the sake of illustrating and confirming the truth, he may have added in the fourteenth Homily the passage respecting baptism. He lived at a time when, in other countries besides Africa,

---

Persarum, verbi gratia, regnum, Indorumque monstraverit · sed ostendat ei omnia regna mundi, id est, regnum suum quomodo regnaret in mundo, ut cohortans eum facere quod velebat, inciperet etiam Christum habere subjectum. Vis, inquit, in hominibus his regnare? [Ostendit innumerabiles hominum multitudines, quæ suo tenebantur imperio. Et revera si miseriam et infelicitatem nostram, simpliciter volumus confiteri, pene totius mundi rex Diabolus est: unde et princeps istius sæculi à salvatore vocatur. Quod ergo dicit: Vides hos homines qui sub meo regno sunt: ostendit ei in puncto temporis, hoc est, in præsenti temporum cursu, qui ad comparationem æternitatis puncti instar obtinet. Neque enim necessarium habuit Salvator, ut ei dignitates sæculi istius et negotia monstrarentur: statim ut aciem luminum suorum ad contemplandum vertit, et peccata regnantia, et eos qui regnarentur à vitiis conspexit, et ipsum principem sæculi Diabolum supervenientem, atque gaudentem in propriam perniciem, quia tantos sub suo habebat imperio.] Nolo contendas, nolo nitaris, ne habeas ullam in certando molestiam. Unum est quod precor: procidens adora me, et accipe regnum omne quod teneo. Verum Dominus noster atque Salvator vult quidem regnare, et omnes gentes subjectas esse ut serviant justitiæ, veritati, cæterisque virtutibus: sed vult regnare quasi justitia, ut absque labore regnet, ut nihil faciat indecorum, et non vult absque labore subjectus Diabolo coronari, nec sic regnare cæteris, ut ipse regnetur à Diabolo. Unde loquitur ad eum Jesus: Scriptum est, *Dominum Deum tuum adorabis, et ipsi soli servies.*

and beyond all doubt, there were children baptized at so early an age that some queries might very naturally arise as to the cause and propriety of their baptism; and in the passage there is allusion to such

(The tempter) *showed to him all the kingdoms of the world,* and of the men of this world; how some may be governed by lasciviousness; others by avarice; those may be swayed by popular applause; these may be taken by the enticements of form. Nor is it to be thought that, showing to him the kingdoms of the world, he would exhibit the kingdom of the Persians, for example, and of the Indians: but he showed to him all the kingdoms of the world; that is, his kingdom, how he reigned in the world; that, having exhorted him to do what he wished, he might begin to have even Christ subjected. Dost thou desire, he saith, to reign over these men? [He showed the innumerable multitudes of men, which were held by his sovereignty—and in truth if we are willing to confess frankly our misery and unhappiness, the Devil is king of almost the whole world: whence also he is by the Saviour called the prince of this world. Which therefore he said: Thou seest these men who are under my dominion. He showed them to him in a moment of time; that is, in the present course of times, which course is as a moment, in comparison with eternity. For the Saviour had no need that the dignities and affairs of this world should be exhibited to him; immediately as he turned the sight of his eyes to contemplating, he saw both the sins reigning, and those persons who were governed by vices, and the prince himself of this world, the Devil, predominant, and rejoicing to his own destruction, because he had so many under his sovereignty.] I wish not that thou contend; I wish not that thou exert thyself; have no trouble in striving. One thing is what I request; falling

queries "*among the brethren.*" He had the most exalted idea of the efficacy of baptism. Near the end of the first book of his 'Apology,' he mentions as an objection which had been made against him by one of his opposers, that he had said, all sins whatever are remitted in baptism; and he proceeds: Let him hear us again proclaiming, In baptism the old Adam entirely dies, and in baptism the new is raised up with Christ; the earthly perishes, and the supercelestial is born. These things we say . . . *interrogated by the brethren,* we have replied according to our conviction.* "Residing in a monastery, and venerated as an oracle, he could hardly fail of hearing, from his brother monks, many inquiries on this and

---

down, worship me, and receive the whole kingdom that I hold. But our Lord and Saviour wishes indeed to reign, and that all the nations be subjected, that they may serve righteousness, truth, and other virtues: but he wishes to reign as by righteousness, that he may reign without labor, that he may do nothing unbecoming, and he wishes not, being subjected to the Devil without labor, to be crowned; nor so to reign over others that himself be reigned over by the Devil. Wherefore Jesus saith to him: It is written, *Thou shalt worship the Lord thy God, and him only shalt thou serve.*

* Audiat nos iterum proclamantes: veterem Adam in lavacro totum mori; et novum cum Christo in baptismate suscitari: perire choicum, et nasci supercœlestem. Hæc dicimus . . . *interrogati à fratribus,* quid nobis videretur respondimus.

kindred subjects. And it must be acknowledged that the passage in the fourteenth Homily has very much the aspect of a distinct additional remark, suggested by the preceding words of the Homily, and here introduced by Jerome, with his usual freedom, for the special benefit of the inquiring monks.

In regard to the translations by Rufin, also, we have special reason to doubt their presenting correctly and without addition the statements made by Origen. This will be evident when we hear the translator's own declarations. At the close of the Commentary on the Epistle to the Romans, he, in a peroration addressed to Heraclius, adverts to the great labor which devolved upon him in translating into Latin some of the productions of Origen, while he endeavored to supply some things not in the manuscripts, in order to give more completeness to the discussion of various matters. These are his words: "While we desire to supply those things which by Origen in the hearing of the church were finished off extemporaneously, not so much for the purpose of explanation as of edification; as we have done in the Homilies or brief addresses on Genesis and on Exodus, and *especially* in those things which were spoken by him on the book of *Leviticus*, in the style of peroration, but have been translated by us in the form of explanation. Which labor of supplying those things which were wanting we undertook, lest questions touched upon and left (what in the homiletic style of speaking is often done by him) should be distasteful to the Latin reader."*

This he says he had done, and *especially on the Book of Leviticus;* but not on Joshua, Judges, and the thirty-sixth and thirty-seventh, and the thirty-eighth Psalm, where, as he soon informs us, he had merely translated (simpliciter ut invenimus).

But he states that he had found the elaborating of the Commentary on the Epistle to the Romans peculiarly arduous. He had alluded to the causes in the preface : the subject was a deep ocean ; the work itself had been interpolated ; while, on the other hand, some books of it were either entirely lost, or could be found only with the greatest difficulty ; and then the whole, without marring its symmetry and connection, was to be compressed into about half the size of the original work.

He gives us to understand that he had toiled cheerfully, but, after all, was censured by some. He mentions their complaint, and makes reply thus :

---

* Dum supplere cupimus ea quæ ab Origene in auditorio ecclesiæ ex tempore, non tam explanationis, quam ædificationis intentione perorata sunt : sicut in Homiliis sive in oratiunculis in Genesin et in Exodum fecimus, et præcipue in his quae in librum Levitici ab illo quidem perorandi stylo dicta, à nobis verè explanandi specie translata sunt. Quem laborem adimplendi quæ deerant idcirco suscepimus, ne pulsatæ quæestiones et relictæ, quod in Homilitico dicendi genere ab illo sæpè fieri solet, Latino lectori fastidium generarent.

"For they say to me, since very many things among those which you write are regarded as your own, give your name in the title, and write, RUFIN'S *books of Commentary on the Epistle to the Romans;* as also among secular authors, they remark, the title bears the name, not of him who is translated from the Greek, but of the translator. All this, however, they suggest, not from love to me, but from hatred to the author. But I, who have more regard to my conscience than to my name, although I appear to *add some things and fill out what are wanting*, or to abbreviate those which are long, yet do not think it right to steal the title of him who laid the foundations of the work, and furnished materials for constructing the edifice. Let the reader judge, when he shall have examined the work, to whom he may please to ascribe its merit. For I have sought, not the applause of readers, but the benefit of those who are proficients."*

---

* Aiunt enim mihi: In his quæ scribis, quoniam plurima in eis tui operis habentur, da titulum nominis tui, et scribe, Rufini, verbi gratia, in Epistolam ad Romanos explanationum libri, sicut et apud auctores, inquiunt, sæculares non illius qui ex Græco translatus est, sed illius qui transtulit nomen titulus tenet. Hoc autem totum mihi donant non amore mei, sed odio auctoris. Verùm ego qui plus conscientiæ meæ, quam nomini defero, etiam si addere aliqua videor et explere quæ desunt, aut breviare quæ longa sunt, furari tamen titulum ejus qui fundamenta operis jecit. et construendi ædificii materiam præbuit, rectum non puto. Sit sanè in arbitrio legentis, cum opus

Rufin mentions his translations on *Joshua* among those which he had made without additions.* Perhaps, as Dr. Gale suggests, he means to assert this *comparatively* in respect to his other translations. For a portion of Origen's twentieth Homily on Joshua, as preserved in the original Greek and presented in the twelfth chapter of the Philocalia (a selection from some of his works, compiled by Basil the Great and Gregory Nazianzen), is remarkably different from the same portion, as it is presented in Rufin's translation. Here he seems to have proceeded with much of his usual freedom. For example: among other things for which nothing is to be found in the Greek, he inserts the following: "As also the Lord says concerning the little ones of the church, that their angels do always stand in the presence of the Lord beholding his face."†

If he has made additions like this in a book which he intended and professed *merely* to translate, he may well be supposed to have made such additions as he may have thought desirable in the Homilies on Leviticus, one of the works which he has mentioned

probaverit, operis meritum cui velit adscribere. Nobis enim propositum est non plausum legentium, sed fructum proficientium quærere.

* Simpliciter ut invenimus, et non multo cum labore transtulimus

† Sicut et Dominus de parvulis ecclesiæ dicit, quia angeli eorum semper assistunt in conspectu Domini, videntes faciem ejus.

"especially," as having been prepared by him in this free manner for the use of Latin readers.

In translating the Commentary on the Epistle to the Romans, while he abridged the original work as a whole, he at least occasionally made additions and alterations. This is evident not only from what he has himself said, but also from a comparison of his version of the Commentary, book i. 2, and book vi. 8, with the Greek in the Philocalia, chapter xxv. and chapter ix. These passages are exhibited, at full length, in the Benedictine edition of Origen's works; and Rufin's version is censured as being unfaithful.*

But we wish to fix the attention of our readers on what he himself has said in the passages which we have presented from his "peroration" and his preface to his translation of the Commentary. Let us think of the impressions under which, manifestly, some of his contemporaries assailed the work. "For they say to me," he remarks, "since very many things among those which you write are regarded as your own, give your name in the title, and write RUFIN's *books of Commentary on the Epistle to the Romans.*" Let us next observe the manner in which he replies. Instead of denying that very many things in the work are his own, he proceeds thus: "But I, who have more regard to my conscience than to my name, although I appear to *add some things and fill out what are wanting,* or to abbreviate those which are long, yet do

* See vol. iv., pp. 462–4, and pp. 580, 581.

not think it right to steal the title of him who laid the foundations of the work and furnished the materials for constructing the edifice."

Here every reader may see for himself that in reference to this work, Rufin speaks of adding some things and filling out what were wanting, as well as of abbreviating those which were long. We need not, therefore, expatiate on the remarkable and important error into which Mr. Wall has fallen in affirming of Rufin that in reference to the Commentary, "he speaks of no addition."

It will be perceived that we do not here bring against the translator any accusation of intending to deceive his readers; but the manner that he adopted, and that he frankly avows, of intermingling some things of his own with those of the author, prevents these translations from having a rightful claim to be regarded as testimonies coming down to us from the age in which the author lived. The additions, whatever they may be, belong to the time, not of the author, but of the translator; and the work in Greek, except a few fragments, having perished, it is now impossible to determine, with certainty, what was derived from the original, and what was added. If a statement harmonizes better with what is known of the time or the character of the translator than with what is known of the time or the character of the author, there arises, of course, a probability that it is an addition.

Origen seems generally to be contented with his

own reasoning in connection with Holy Scripture. Rufin is less independent. Looking back from about the close of the fourth century, he would be very likely to speak of ecclesiastical usage, and to think of a certain precept as being pertinent in relation to children; for in the so-called Apostolical Constitutions, which had then been in circulation a hundred years, it is enjoined: "*Moreover, baptize your children, and bring them up in the nurture and admonition of the Lord; for he saith, Suffer the little children to come unto me, and forbid them not.*"* (Book vi. ch. 15.)

That the first six books of the work claiming to be the Constitutions of the Holy Apostles, were written in the latter part of the third century, and hence after the time of Origen, yet so early as we have assumed, has been sufficiently proved in the Prize Essay on their origin and contents, appended to Appleton's edition (New York, 1848), and by Von Drey, a Professor in the Catholic Theological Faculty at Tübingen, in his New Investigations—*Neue Untersuchungen über die Constitutionem, etc.* In respect to some parts of the work, an earlier time, with some original views, is advocated by the distinguished author of the work on Hippolytus and his Age. The case before us does not require and our limits forbid any attempt here to discuss the point.

---

* Book vi., ch. 15. *Βαπτίζετε δὲ υμῶν καὶ τὰ νήπια, καὶ ἐκτρέφετε αὐτὰ ἐν παιδέιᾳ καὶ νουθεσίᾳ θεοῦ· ἄφετε γὰρ φησὶ τὰ παιδία ἐρχέσθαι πρός με, καὶ μὴ κωλύετε αὐτά.*

In view of the facts which we have been stating, we do not see how it can fairly be denied that the passages which have been urged as coming from Origen are far from being of the most reliable character. Perhaps a just historical criticism would discriminate, and mark the more doubtful parts with brackets.

HOMILY VIII. ON LEVITICUS, (ch. 12 : 1–8.)

According to Rufin's Latin version.

Hear David speaking: *I was*, says he, *conceived in iniquity, and in sin did my mother bring me forth;* showing that every soul that is born in the flesh is polluted with the filth of iniquity and sin; and that, therefore, that was said which we mentioned before, that *none is clean from pollution, though his life be but of the length of one day.* [To these considerations it can be added, that it may be inquired why, since the baptism of the church is given for the remission of sins, baptism is given, according to the observance of the church, even to children; for the grace of baptism would seem superfluous if there were nothing in children requiring remission and indulgence.]*

* Audi David dicentem : In iniquitatibus, inquit, conceptus sum, et in peccatis peperit me mater mea; ostendens quod quæcunque anima in carne nascatur, iniquitatis et peccati sorde polluitur; et propterea dictum esse illud quod jam superius memoravimus, quia nemo mundus à sorde, nec si unius diei fuerit vita ejus. [Addi his etiam illud potest, ut requiratur quid causæ sit, cum baptisma ecclesiæ in remissionem peccatorum detur, secundum ecclesiæ observantiam etiam parvulis baptismum dari; cum utique si

HOMILY XIV. ON LUKE, (ch. 2 : 21–24.)

According to Jerome's Latin version.

[Having occasion given in this place, I touch again upon what is frequently inquired about among the brethren. Children are baptized for the remission of sins. Of what sins? or when have they sinned? or how can any reason of the laver in their case hold good, unless according to that sense which we have just now mentioned? *None is free from pollution, though his life be but of the length of one day upon the earth.* And because, through the sacrament of baptism, the pollution of nativity is removed, therefore children also are baptized. For *unless any one be born of water and of the Spirit, he will not be able to enter into the kingdom of heaven.*]*

COMMENTARY ON THE EPISTLE TO THE ROMANS, BOOK V., 9.

According to Rufin's Latin version.

And also in the law it is commanded that a sacrifice be offered for the child that is born; *a pair of turtle-doves, or*

---

nihil esset in parvulis quod ad remissionem deberet et in dulgentiam pertinere, gratia baptismi superflua videretur.]

* Quod frequenter inter fratres quæritur, loci occasione commotus retracto. Parvuli baptizantur in remissionem peccatorum. Quorum peccatorum? vel quo tempore peccaverunt? Aut quomodo potest ulla lavacri in parvulis ratio subsistere, nisi juxta illum sensum de quo paulo ante diximus: *nullus mundus à sorde, nec si unius diei quidem fuerit vita ejus super terram?* Et quia per baptismi sacramentum nativitatis sordes deponuntur, propterea baptizantur et parvuli. *Nisi enim quis renatus fuerit ex aqua et spiritu, non poterit intrare in regnum cœlorum.*]

two young pigeons; of which one is for a sin-offering, the other for a burnt-offering. For what sin is this one pigeon offered? Can the new-born child have committed any sin? and yet it has sin, for which the sacrifice is commanded to be offered, and from which even he *whose life is but of one day* is denied to be free. Of this sin, therefore, David is to be supposed to have said that which we mentioned before, *In sin did my mother conceive me;* for no sin of his mother is affirmed in history. [For this also the church has received a tradition from the apostles to give baptism even to children; for they to whom the secrets of the divine mysteries were committed, knew that in all persons there is the native pollution of sin, which must be done away by the water and the Spirit; on account of which pollution, even the body itself is called the body of sin.]*

If Jerome and Rufin added the sentences included

---

* Denique et in lege pro illo qui natus fuerit, jubetur offerri hostia, par turturum aut duo pulli columbini; ex quibus unus pro peccato, alius in holocantomata. Pro quo peccato offertur hic pullus unus? Numquid nuper editus parvulus peccare jam potuit? Et tamen habet peccatum pro quo hostia jubetur offerri, à quo mundus negatur quis esse, nec si unius diei fuerit vita ejus. De hoc ergo etiam David dixisse credendus est illud quod supra memoravimus: quia *in peccatis concepit me mater mea.* Secundum historiam enim nullum matris ejus declaratur peccatum. [Pro hoc et ecclesia ab apostolis traditionem suscepit, etiam parvulis baptismum dare. Sciebant enim illi quibus mysteriorum secreta commissa sunt divinorum, quod essent in omnibus genuinæ sordes peccati, quæ per aquam et Spiritum ablui deberent; propter quas etiam corpus ipsum corpus peccati nominatur.]

in brackets, they did only what was in accordance with their avowed manner in these translations; and they expressed themselves as they naturally would have done in the time and circumstances in which they lived. But whether they actually added these sentences from their own resources or translated them from Origen, we do not affirm; for we have not the means of knowing. Certainly Du Pin had too much reason to say as he does, after speaking of Rufin's translations, that "Jerome's are not more exact." Erasmus uttered only the plain truth, when he indignantly remarked that the reader is "uncertain whether he reads Origen or Rufin." And Dr. Redepenning, a Theological Professor in the University of Göttingen, who, within a few years, has published an elaborate and highly esteemed work on the Life and Teaching of Origen, in speaking of the Commentary on the Epistle to the Romans, as we have it from Rufin, characterizes it as being *intermediate between a translation and a treatise: a reproduction adapted to the views and wants of the later age in which it was prepared.**

But these considerations in regard to Jerome and Rufin we need not urge. They belong, however, to

---

* So ist sein Werk ein Mittleres zwischen Übersetzung und Bearbeitung, eine Wiedererzeugung nach Massgabe der Ansichten und Bedürfnisse des späteren Jahrhunderts. See Redepenning's *Origenes: eine Darstellung seines Lebens und seiner Lehre.* Vol. ii., p. 190.

he subject, and ought not to be overlooked; especially if the passages in question are to be understood as teaching what they have commonly been thought to teach, and what, as we hope soon to show, would be far more likely to be taught by Jerome and Rufin, even in using the same words, near the close of the fourth century, than by Origen, a hundred and fifty years before.

Even if the words that mention *apostolic tradition* be supposed to have come from Origen, be it so. The expression, Neander assures us, "can not be regarded as of much weight in that age, when the inclination was so strong to trace to the apostles every institution which was considered of special importance; and when so many walls of separation, hindering the freedom of prospect, had already been set up between that and the apostolic age."* But these pertinent considerations, too, we need not urge.

Even if the usage or observance mentioned be supposed to have existed in the time of Origen, and to have been in accordance with the reputed teaching of the apostles, be it so. The inquiry then arises, What was the usage mentioned? Who are spoken of as being baptized? Are they infants, as Mr. Wall and many others translate the word (parvuli), in the sense which we commonly attach to the word infants? Are they unconscious babes? Not

* Neander's General History of the Christian Religion and Church, vol. i., p. 314.

at all. They are children, such as, in our day, might be found in the Sunday-school, young children, instructed in the first principles of the doctrine of Christ, and professing Christian faith and obedience.

Even the Latin word *infans*, infant, with the literally corresponding Greek, νήπιος, it is well known, is often used with much latitude of signification. According to the nature of the discourse and of the connection, it may be spoken of a child at any time from his birth to the close of his minority. An illustration of this remark, with respect to the Greek, may be found in the apostle Paul's Epistle to the Galatians, 4 : 1 : Now I say that the heir, as long as he is a child, νήπιος, differeth nothing from a servant, though he be lord of all; but is under tutors and governors until the time appointed of the father.

We are aware that, in order to support infant baptism, Mr. Wall, in his History, part i., chapter v., introduces a passage from the ninth Homily on Joshua, in the course of which these words occur: "And thou wast an infant in baptism."* That Origen means an infant, not in age, but in a figurative sense, is manifest from the consideration that he proceeds to speak of our Saviour's writing his law on the heart at the time. Of course, one would think, it must have been a heart that could receive and

* Et tu fuisti infans in baptismo.

understand. That this is the true sense is more abundantly evident from the subsequent remarks of Origen, which Mr. Wall has not quoted. These show clearly that the writing is connected with instruction and faith. It is *in the hearts of believers** that the new law is written. Origen says expressly: "But even now by these things which we speak, Jesus writes the second law in the hearts of those who, with sound faith and the whole mind, receive those truths which are proclaimed."†

In reference to the little ones connected with the congregation of Israel, as mentioned in Josh. 8: 35, Origen speaks also in his ninth Homily on that book; but he says not one word favorable to baptizing unconscious babes. On the contrary, he remarks, section 9, in making out, after his manner, a parallel under the new dispensation: "But the infants will be those who, having recently believed, are nourished with the evangelical milk.‡

The word employed in the passages under consideration, *parvuli*, little ones, children, is also, in itself, indefinite; and it is sometimes interchanged with other words indicating children. Its usual meaning,

* In cordibus credentium.

† Sed et nunc per hæc quæ loquimur, Jesus deuterono mium scribit in eorum cordibus qui integra fide et toto animo quæ dicuntur accipiunt.

‡ Infantes vero erunt, qui fide nuper suscepta, lacte evangelico nutriuntur.

and its being freely interchanged, are both strikingly illustrated in Origen's nineteenth Homily on Luke, as translated by Jerome; where the word in the singular number, parvulus, is used as the leading designation of our Lord, at the time when, in his childhood, he went up to Jerusalem. The passage to which we allude is the following: "Not when he came to the age of youth [adolescentiam, the period from the fifteenth to the thirtieth year]; not when he entered publicly on the work of teaching, but when he was yet a child, *parvulus*, he had the favor of God: and, as all things in him had been wonderful, so also his childhood, *pueritia*, was wonderful, so that he was filled with the wisdom of God. . . . When, therefore, as we have said, he was twelve years old, and, according to custom, the days of the solemnity were completed, and his parents would return with the little child, *infantulus*, Jesus, the lad, *puer*, remained in Jerusalem, and his parents knew it not. . . . . It was impossible that she [Mary, after what had been revealed to her] should fear the infant, *infans*, was utterly lost. . . . But when he was a child, *parvulus*, he is found in the midst of the doctors, sanctifying them and imbuing, them with knowledge. Because he was a child, *parvulus*, he is found in the midst, not teaching them, but interrogating; and this as being suitable to his age, that he might teach us what is suitable for lads, *pueris*, although they may be wise and learned; namely, that they should hear masters, rather than desire to teach or become vain and ostentatious."*

Here it is most manifest that one who was twelve years of age is repeatedly called *parvulus*, and that the word, in its general purport, corresponds well with the English word *child*.

Irenæus, in his work against Heresies, near the close of the second century, dividing the human family into five classes according to the different periods of life, mentions *parvulos*, children, after *infantes*, infants, and before *pueros*, lads or youths, as the words are commonly used among us. He places *parvulos* in a position intermediate between the period of infancy and the period of youth; that is, he places them in the *later* and perhaps larger portion of

* Non quando venit ad adolescentiam, non quando manifeste docebat, sed cum adhuc esset *parvulus* habebat gratiam Dei: et quomodo omnia in illo mirabilia fuerant, ita et *pueri ia* mirabilis fuit, ut Dei sapientia compleretur. . . . . Cum ergo, ut diximus, duodecim esset annorum, et juxta morem dies solemnitatis expleti essent, et reverterentur parentes cum *infantulo* Jesu, remansit *puer* in Jerusalem, et nesciebant parentes ejus. . . . Nunquam fieri poterat ut perditum formidaret *infantem*. . . . Quoniam verò *parvulus* erat, invenitur in medio præceptorum, sanctificans et erudiens eos. Quia *parvulus* erat, invenitur in medio, non eos docens, sed interrogans, et hoo pro ætatis officio; ut nos doceret quid *pueris*, quamvis sapientes et eruditi sint, conveniret, ut audiant potius magistros, quam docere, desiderent, et se vana ostentatione non jactent.

childhood; and he speaks of Christ as being *to them an example* of piety, uprightness and obedience *

On this topic it would seem unnecessary to say more. In itself the word *parvuli,* like many others, is somewhat indefinite, as we have already remarked; and therefore it is liable to be misunderstood; but, viewed in the light of the undeniable statements which we have now made, and of the facts well known in the time of Origen, its meaning is sufficiently clear.

If it be objected that the native pollution of the child, the reason assigned for his needing the remission of sin, is applicable to his case from the time of his birth, and therefore he should be baptized without delay, even in unconscious infancy; we reply that such was the reasoning of subsequent Fathers, but not of Origen. He kept in mind what was required of every one in order to be baptized and receive remission. According to his system, the same native pollution, whatever it was, that adhered to the newborn child, adhered also to the unbaptized adult; and yet the adult was not to be baptized immediately. He was first to be instructed. He was to be told of Christ, that he might believe on him; for such faith the gospel required. He was to be taught the elements of the true religion, that he might know and

* Infantes, et *parvulos,* et pueros, et juvenes, et seniores . . . Christ came in parvulis parvulus, sanctificans hanc ipsam habentes ætatem; simul et *exemplum illis* pietatis effectus, et justitiæ, et subjectionis. Lib. ii., c. 22 § 4.

love the truth which he was to profess in baptism, and that he might honor it by a holy life. He was to be baptized, when, in Christian knowledge, disposition and deportment, he seemed to be a suitable person. Why could not Origen have supposed that the same principle was to be applied to the case of children? He thought much of the preparation required of every one in order to be benefitted by baptism, as a grand and blessed remedy for sin. Subsequent Fathers thought so much of the remedy as to deem it efficacious, even without the preparation.

Another fact also it is important to remember. Origen maintained that sin is not imputed to children, till they come to years of discretion. In his Commentary on the Epistle to the Romans, he says:

"Until the natural law, sin is dead. Therefore at a certain time of age, when any one begins to be capable of reason, and to have discernment of just and unjust, of right and wrong, then sin, which before was within the person as dead, is said to revive; because there is now within him a law which forbids, and there is reason which shows that the thing ought not to be done. But that what we say may be more clearly understood, let us use a plain example. It is written: '*He that smiteth his father or his mother, shall surely be put to death; and he that curseth his father or his mother, shall surely be put to death.*' [Lev. xxi : 15 and 17.] Now a little boy of about four or five years, if, displeased, as often occurs, he smite with a rod his father or his mother, deserves according to the statute, to die. But, since there is not yet in him the natural law which may teach him that he ought not to do injury to his father or to his mother, and since he knows not that in this is involved the crime of impiety, what he does is indeed a species of sin, because he smites or curses his father or his mother: but in him sin is dead, because through the absence of the natural law which is not yet in him sin cannot be imputed to him. For there is not yet within him so much reason as to teach him that this which he does ought not to be done; and therefore by his parents it is not only not reckoned as a fault, but is received as a pleasant act."*

* Usque ad legem enim naturalem, peccatum mortuum est. Ergo certo ætatis tempore ubi rationis capax esse quis cæperit. et justi injustique, æqui et iniqui habere discrimen, tunc peccatum, quod priùs intra hominem velut mortaum habebatur, reviviscere dicitur, pro eo quòd est jam intrinsecus lex quæ vetet, et ratio quæ ostendat non esse faciendum. Sed ut apertius intelligatur quod dicimus, evidenti utamur exemplo. Scriptum est: *Qui percusserit patrem, vel matrem, morte moriatur;* et *Qui male dixerit patri, aut matri, morte moriatur.* Puer ergo parvulus quatuor ferè aut quinque annorum si (ut fieri solet) indignatus virga percutiat patrem aut matrem, quantum ad præceptum mandati spectat, mortem debet. Sed quia lex in illo nondum est naturalis, quæ eum doceat non debere injuriam facere patri aut matri, nec in hoc crimen impietatis admitti; est quidem species peccati quod facit; quia percutit patrem vel matrem, aut maledicit; sed mortuum est in eo peccatum, quia per absentiam naturalis legis, quæ in eo non-

In this passage, Origen does not attempt to state precisely when children arrive at the period of clear moral discernment and accountability; but from what he says it is evident that he supposed it to be at least some time *after* "four or five years," or, in other words, *not before* entering the sixth year. And it is remarked by a distinguished European medical author that "the *seventh* year, and the vicinity of each multiple of seven, is characterized by some great change in the human constitution. Thus the seventh year is that of the second dentition, and *the common belief fixes at that age the distinct perception of right and wrong.*"*

Moreover, according to Origen's teaching, it is not *before*, but *when* the child comes to the discernment of right and wrong, that he can be made capable of receiving the grace of Christ. By the expression here used, the grace of Christ, he seems to mean the benefits which Christ graciously bestows on decided believers in connection with their being baptized. Our readers may wish to see the whole passage to which we allude. We give it entire, and leave it with them to judge of its bearing on the topic before us. It occurs in the Commentary on the Epistle to the

---

dum est, peccatum ei non potest reputari. Nondum est enim intra eum ratio tanta quæ eum doceat hoc quod facit, fieri non debere: et ideo etiam à parentibus non solùm non reputatur ad culpam, sed ad gratiam jucunditatemque suscipitur.

* Tilt's Elements of Health, p. 21.

Romans, book v., 2. Remarking on the eighteenth verse of the fifth chapter, Origen proceeds thus:

"But perhaps thou wilt say, If, one sinning, death came upon all men, and again the righteousness of one came upon all men as justification unto life, neither is any thing done by us that we die, or that we live, but Adam causes our death, and Christ our life.

"We have indeed already stated that parents not only generate but also instruct children. And they who are born become not only children but also disciples of their parents; and they are urged to the death connected with sin, not so much by nature as by education. For example: If any one departing from God, worship idols, will he not early teach his children to venerate idols, and offer sacrifices to demons? This the child does according to Adam; that is, from his nativity to the time of the law, when, *coming to the discernment of right and wrong, he can be made capable of receiving the grace of Christ.* And there he leaves Adam, who either generated or taught him unto death, and follows Christ, who both teaches and generates unto life.

"Dost thou wish to know why it is not only from nativity but also from teaching that death has reigned from Adam? Learn this from the contrary. For the Lord Jesus Christ, when he came to repair what had rashly been done, since that first nativity which came from Adam would generate unto death, introduced a second nativity, which he has called not so much generation as regeneration, through which, doubtless, he would abolish the fault of the first nativity; and as he substituted regeneration for generation, so also he substituted another teaching for the former teaching. For, sending forth his disciples to this work, he said not merely, Go, baptize all nations; but he saith, Go, teach all nations, baptizing them in the name of the Father, and of the Son, and of the Holy Ghost. Knowing therefore that each is in fault, he gave a remedy for each, that the mortal generation might be changed by the regeneration of baptism, and that the teaching of piety might exclude the teaching of impiety. Not therefore to us doing nothing has death reigned in us; as, on the other hand, not to us idle and doing nothing will life reign in us. But indeed the beginning of life is given by Christ, not to the unwilling, but to the believing; and we arrive at perfection of life by perfection of virtues; as also we hasten to death by similitude of transgression and the practice of vices."*

* Sed dices fortasse: Si uno peccante mors in omnes homines pertransiit, et rursus unius justitia in omnes homines justificatio vitæ pervenit, neque ut moreremur aliquid nobis gestum est, neque ut vivamus, sed est mortis quidem causa Adam, vitæ autem Christus.

Diximus quidem jam et in superioribus, quòd parentes non solùm generant filios, sed et imbuunt: et qui nascuntur, non solùm filii parentibus, sed et discipuli fiunt, et non tam natura urgentur in mortem peccati, quàm disciplina. Verbi causa enim, si quis à Deo recedens idola estat, nonne continuò etiam filios si genuerit docebit idola vener-

In these remarks there are several points that can hardly fail to arrest and fix the attention; first, a maturity sufficient for moral discernment as being necessary to a child's having capacity or being in a state for receiving the remission of sin; next, instruc-

ùri, et sacrificia offerre dæmoniis? Hoc secundùm Adam facit, hoc est, à nativitate usque ad agis tempus, quo ad discretionem recti pravique operis veniens, capax Christi gratiæ effici potest: et ibi relinquit Adam qui eum vel genuit vel docuit in mortem, et sequitur Christum, qui eum et docet et gignit ad vitam.

Vis autem scire quia non solùm nativitatis, sed et doctrinæ est, in quo mors regnavit ab Adam? Disce hoc et contrariis. Etiam Dominus Jesus Christus cùm venissit quæ perperàm gesta fuerant emendare, pro eo quòd in mortem generaret illa quæ ex Adam veniebat prima nativitas, introduxit secundam nativitatem, quam non tam generationem quam regenerationem appellavit, per quam sine dubio vitium primæ nativitatis aboleret: et sicut generationi substituit regenerationem, ita et doctrinæ substituit aliam doctrinam. Mittens enim ad hoc opus discipulos suos, non dixit tantùm. Ite, baptizate omnes gentes; sed ait, Ite, docete omnes gentes, baptizantes eos in nomine Patris, et Filii, et Spiritus Sancti. Sciens igitur utrumque esse in culpa, utrique remedium dedit, ut generatio mortalis regeneratione baptismi mutaretur, et impietatis doctrinam doctrina pietatis excluderet. Non ergo nihil peccantibus nobis mors regnavit in nobis: sicut rursum non otiosis nobis, et nihil agentibus vita regnabit in nobis. Sed initium quidem vitæ datur à Christo, non invitis, sed credentibus; et pervenitur ad perfectionem vitæ perfectione virtutum, sicut et in mortem dudum prævaricationis similitudine et vitiorum expletione perventum est.

tion as well as baptism, and preceding it, not merely, Go, baptize, but Go, teach, baptizing ; and then the great pervading principle so emphatically stated, that the *beginning* of spiritual life, as well as its progress, is given by Christ, not to the idle, the careless, and indifferent, nor to the unwilling, but *to them that believe.*

Now, what we maintain is, that if Origen speaks in the passages so often quoted, as coming from him, in support of infant baptism, he ought to be understood as referring to the baptism of children of sufficient age to be conscious moral agents. This explanation might be still further confirmed by a survey of the earliest ecclesiastical formularies and other ancient documents that have come down to us, whether as apostolical constitutions, or in some other form. But it is not our design now to exhibit any of these. We have confirmation more direct. We have Origen's own testimony, showing when children were to be baptized.

In his work against Celsus, book iii., chapter 59, a passage is quoted from Celsus, in which, after mentioning what intelligent and respectable persons are invited to initiation in the sacred mysteries among the heathen, this acute and bitter adversary of Christianity proceeds thus :

" And now let us hear what persons the Christians invite. Whoever, they say, is a sinner, whoever is unintelligent, whoever is a mere child, and in short

whoever is a miserable and contemptible creature, the kingdom of God shall receive him."*

Origen then subjoins: "In reply to these accusations we say, It is one thing to invite those who are diseased in the soul to a healing, and it is another to invite the healthy to a knowledge and discernment of things more divine. And we, knowing the difference, first call men to be healed. We exhort sinners to come to the instruction that teaches them not to sin, and the unintelligent to come to that which produces in them understanding, and *the little children to rise in elevation of thought to the man*, and the miserable to come to a fortunate state, or (what is more proper to say) a state of happiness. But when those of the exhorted that make progress show that they have been cleansed by the word, and, as much as possible, have lived a better life, THEN we invite them to be initiated among us."†

To be initiated among the Christians, it is well

---

* Ὑπακόυσωμεν δὲ τίνας ποτὲ ὄυτοι καλὄυσιν· ὄστις (φησὶν) ἁμαρτωλὸς, ὅστις ἀσύνετος, ὅστις νήπιος, καὶ ὡς ἁπλῶς εἰπεῖν, ὅστις κακοδάιμων· τοῦτον ἡ βασιλεία τοῦ θεοῦ δέξεται.

† Πρὸς ταῦτα δὲ φαμεν, ὅτι οὐ ταὐτον ἐστι νοσοῦντας τὴν ψυχὴν ἐπὶ θεραπείαν καλεῖν, καὶ ὑγιάινοντας ἐπὶ τὴν τῶν θειοτέρων γνῶσιν καὶ ἐπιστήμην. Καὶ ἡμεῖς δὲ ἀμφότερα ταῦτα γιγνώσκοντες, κατ' ἀρχὴν μὲν προκαλὄυμενοι ἐπὶ τὸ θεραπευθῆναι τοὺς ἀνθρώπους προτρέπομεν τοὺς ἁμαρτωλὸυς ἥκειν ἐπὶ τὸυς διδάσκοντας λόγους μὴ ἁμαρτάνειν, καὶ τοὺς ἀσυνέτους ἐπὶ τὸυς ἐμποιοῦντας σύνεσιν, καὶ τὸυς νηπίους εἰς τὸ ἀναβαίνειν φρονήματι ἐπὶ τὸν ἄνδρα, καὶ τὸυς ἁπλῶς κακοδαίμονας ἐπὶ ἐυδαιμονίαν, ἢ (ὅπερ κυριώτερόν ἐστιν εἰπεῖν) ἐπὶ μακαριότητα. Ἐπὰν δ' οἱ προκόπτοντες τῶν προτραπέντων παραστήσωσι τὸ κεκαθάρθαι ὑπὸ τοῦ λόγου, καὶ, ὅση δύναμις, βέλτιον βεβιωκέναι· τὰ τηνικάδε καλοῦμεν αὐτοὺς ἐπὶ τὰς παρ ἡμῖν τελετάς.

known, was to be admitted to baptism and the Lord's supper. In this passage, the testimony of Origen is remarkably explicit. It needs no lengthened comment. The reader himself sees at once the little children, as well as the rest, the *little children*, the *parvuli*, or whatever other endearing name they may bear, were exhorted in a way adapted to their character; and when those of the exhorted who make progress show that they have been cleansed by the word, and, as much as possible, have lived a better life, *then* they are admitted to baptism. Celsus reproaches the Christians for receiving to their fellowship certain classes of the population. Origen replies triumphantly, with express reference to each class, and states when, or on what condition, any are admitted.

We would render devout thanks to God that, under his good and ever-watchful providence, this passage has been preserved from the ravages of time. Here it stands, an authentic record in the original Greek. Henceforth let its light shine on what has long been a much obscured place in ecclesiastical antiquity.

In the next chapter, Origen represents the candidate for Christian initiation as one who has come to the healing of the word,* that is, to be healed by evangelical teaching; one who has been cleansed in the soul, and who loves the Saviour sincerely. In this connection he says, "Let him with cheerful

* Προσελήλυθε τῇ τοῦ λόγου θεραπείᾳ.

countenance be initiated into the mysteries of the religion of Jesus, which, with good reason, are delivered to those only who are holy and pure."* Setting forth the holiness and purity required by the Christian religion, he says, in his third Homily on Genesis, section 5 : "This is the circumcision with which the Church of Christ circumcises the ears of her infants. These, I think, are the ears which he required in his hearers, saying, *Who hath ears to hear let him hear.* For no one with uncircumcised and impure ears can hear the pure words of wisdom and truth.† And in his eighth Homily on Exodus, section 4, he adds : For there dwelt in us an impure spirit before we believed—before we came to Christ. . . . . We have therefore been received by Christ, and our house has been purified from the former sins, and adorned with the ornaments of the believers' sacraments, *which they have known who have been initiated.*"‡

The Christian mysteries, the sacraments, for this

---

* . . . . *ϑάῤῥων μυέισϑω τὰ μόνοις ἁγιοῖς καὶ καϑαρδις εὐλόγως παραδιδόμενα μυστήρια τῆς κατὰ Ιησδυν ϑεοσεβείας.*

† Hæc est circumcisio, qua ecclesia Christi aures suorum circumcidit infantum. Istæ credo sunt aures, quas in auditoribus suis requirebat, dicens : *Qui habet aures audiendi audiat.* Nemo enim potest incircumcisis et immundis auribus munda verba sapientiæ et veritatis audire.

‡ Habitavit enim in nobis immundus spiritus, antequam crederemus, antequam veniremus ad Christum. . . . Suscepti ergo sumus à Christo, et mundata est domus nostra a peccatis prioribus, et ornata est ornamentis sacramentorum fidelium, *quæ norunt qui initiati sunt.*

is the signification of the word mysteries, where Origen speaks of being initiated with cheerful countenance, he says are with good reason for those only who are pure ; and now, including himself with his hearers—himself, the much loved son of Christian parents—he states, "There dwelt in us an impure spirit before we believed." Therefore, manifestly, he teaches that, before he and those whom he was addressing believed, they were not prepared to receive the symbol of having been purified; and it would have been wrong to confer on them the believers' sacraments. Besides, it is difficult to conceive how he could have made the unqualified remark with which the last quotation ends, if some and even many, when they were initiated, were not of sufficient age to have any knowledge of those sacraments.

In the twelfth Homily on Numbers, section 4, he further adds: "Let *each one* of the believers recall to mind what words he there used at that time when he first came to the waters of baptism, when he received the first symbols of the faith, and approached the salutary fountain; and how he renounced the devil, that he would not use his pomps, nor his works, nor comply at all with any of his services and pleasures."*

* Recordetur *unusquisque* fidelium, cum primum venit ad aquas baptismi, cum signacula fidei prima suscepit, et ad fontem salutarem accessit, quibus ibi tunc usus sit verbis, et quid renunciaverit diabolo: non se usurum pompis ejus,

How, in view of such an appeal as this, can we deny that *each one* of the believers was expected to be *able* to remember the solemn scene of his baptism? And if each could remember his own baptism, and what he said and what he did at the time, surely he could not then have been a mere infant.

Speaking of the linen girdle mentioned in Jeremiah xiii : 1–11, Origen says, in his eleventh Homily, section 6, on that book: "But why also *linen?* Because it has its generation from the earth. For a plant springs up from the earth; then, after being cultivated, it is combed, and washed and cleansed, and, with much effort, made suitable for a girdle or other use. And so we *all* have the generation as a girdle of God; and having the generation from much careful preparation, we need that we should be combed, that we should be washed, that we should cast away the color of the earth. For the color of the generation of the flax is different from the color which arises from effort. The color of the generation of the flax is dark, but from effort it becomes most splendid. And such a change comes upon us who are generated. We are black at the commencement of our believing. Wherefore at the commencement of the Song of Songs it is said, I am black, but comely. And at first we are like Ethiopians as to the soul; then we are cleansed, so that we may become more splendid (according to the passage,

neque operibus ejus, neque ullis omnino servitiis ejus ac voluntatibus pariturum.

Who is this that cometh up, made white ?) and may be linen splendid and pure. And then we are woven upon the girdle of God, when we become suitable to be joined to God. . . . . This girdle is the church which is from the Gentiles ; that is, the Christian church, now the people of God instead of the Jews ; who, as a nation, were cast off, according to the representation in the context."*

Here Origen has taken occasion to describe, in his favorite manner, his views respecting the natural state of mankind, and the reformatory process through which every one must pass, in order to participate in the character and privileges of the church. And so we ALL have the generation as a girdle of God. It is "from much careful preparation." At first, when we begin to believe, we are of a dark color ; but at length we are changed. We become linen, splendid and pure. And *then* we are woven upon the girdle

* Διὰ τί δὲ καὶ λινοῦν; ὅτι τὴν γένεσιν ἔχει ἀπὸ γῆς· φυτὸν γάρ ἐστιν ἀνατέλλον ἀπὸ γῆς, εἶτα μετὰ τὸ γεωργηθῆναι ξαινόμενον, καὶ πολλῇ ἐργασίᾳ γινόμενον ἵνα γένηται τοιοῦτον ὥστε γινέσθαι περίζωμα, ἤ ὅτι δήποτε, καὶ ἡμεῖς οὖν πάντες τὴν γένεσιν ἔχομεν ὡς περίζωμα τοῦ θεοῦ. καὶ ἔχοντες τὴν γένεσιν ἀπὸ τῆς πολλῆς κατασκευῆς, χρῄζομεν ἵνα ξανθῶμεν, ἵνα πλυνθῶμεν, ἵνα τὸ χρῶμα τῆς γῆς ἀποβάλωμεν· ἄλλο γὰρ τὸ τῆς γενέσεως τοῦ λινοῦ χρῶμα, ἄλλο τὸ ἀπὸ τῆς ἐργασίας. τὸ μὲν γὰρ τῆς γενέσεως τοῦ λινοῦ χρῶμα μελανότερον ἐστιν, ἀπὸ δὲ τῆς ἐργασίας γίνεται λαμπρότατον. τοιοῦτον οὖν τι καὶ ἐπὶ ἡμᾶς τοὺς ἐν γενέσει φθάνει. μέλανες ἐσμὲν κατὰ τὴν ἐν τῷ πιστεύειν ἀρχήν διὸ ἐν ἀρχῇ τοῦ ᾄσματος τῶν ᾀσμάτων λέγεται· μέλαινά εἰμι, καὶ καλή. καὶ Αἰθίοψιν ἡμεῖς κατ' ἀρχὰς τὴν ψυχήν ἐδικαμεν, εἶτα ἀποσμηχόμεθα, ἵνα λαμπρότεροι γενώμεθα, κατὰ τό· τίς ἄυτη ἡ ἀναβαίνουσα λελευκανθισμένη; καὶ γενώμεθα λινοῦν λαμπρὸν καὶ καθαρόν. εἶτα καὶ πλεκόμεθα ἐπὶ τὸ περίζωμα τοῦ θεοῦ, ὅταν ἀξιῶμεν κολλᾶσθαι τῷ θεῷ . . . . Τοῦτο περίζωμα ἡ ἐκκλησία ἐστὶν ἡ ἀπὸ τῶν ἐθνῶν.

of God—this girdle is the church—when we become suitable to be joined to God.

To be "woven upon the girdle of God," it is obvious, must here signify to be incorporated with the church, or initiated into it by baptism. The representation as to the time when any one was to be admitted, it will be perceived, harmonizes remarkably with that which is given in our longest quotation from Origen's work against Celsus; and, in effect, utters the same testimony.

In his Commentary on John, tom. vi., 17, Origen speaks of Matthew's statement that John the Baptist baptized *unto repentance;* and he most explicitly represents Matthew as, by this statement, *teaching that the benefit from baptism depends on the deliberate purpose of the baptized, it belonging indeed to the penitent.**

Origen received with reverence the teachings of the sacred writers. Some deliberate purpose of forsaking sin, it is therefore evident, he himself thought to be required of those who were to be baptized; and hence he must have contemplated them as being of sufficient age to cherish such a purpose. More than once he has said in effect, what he says in his Commentary on the Epistle to the Romans, book v., chapter 8, namely: "If any one is previously dead to sin, he, of course, is buried with Christ; but if any one

* . . . . . *διδάσκων τὸ, ἀπὸ τοῦ βαπτίσματος ὠφέλειαν ἔχεσθαι τῆς προαιρέσεως τοῦ βαπτιζομένου, τῷ μετανοοῦντι μὲν ἐγγινομένην.*

does not before die to sin, he cannot be buried with Christ. For no one, while alive, is buried. But if he is not buried with Christ, neither is he legitimately baptized."*

In presenting the testimony of Origen respecting the baptism of children, we have endeavored to avoid as much as possible all irrelevant matters, and to state with fidelity and clearness what belongs essentially to the subject. We have taken some pains to ascertain the truth. We have examined, for ourselves, the voluminous works of Origen; and we have become thoroughly convinced that the system of infant baptism adopted by subsequent ecclesiastical fathers never entered his mind; although some of his speculations on the pollution connected with nativity, on the passage found only in the Septuagint version, not in the Hebrew original of Job xiv: 4, and on Psalm li: 5, as well as the somewhat indefinite statements attributed to him, claiming the authority of apostolical tradition, may have greatly contributed, at a later period, to the establishment of that system.

The term children, parvuli, was in itself indefinite.

* Si quis priùs mortuus est peccato, is necessariò in baptismo consepultus est: si verò non ante quis moritur peccato, non potest sepeliri cum Christo. Nemo enim vivus aliquando sepelitur. Quòd si non consepelitur Christo, nec legitimè baptizatur.

Various and strong influences, in the third and fourth centuries, were constantly tending to hasten the baptism of children, and make it, strictly and literally, *infant* baptism ; so that we need not wonder if what Origen or a reputed apostolical constitution had said, with some indefiniteness, respecting the baptism of children in the later portion of childhood, without saying precisely what children, soon came to be understood and used by many as sanctioning the baptism of children in their earliest infancy. Many a word, in the lapse of time, has undergone a very considerable change of signification, in consequence of change in the customs of the people.

Pedobaptism, in the most ancient sense of the word, the baptism of children capable of professing their faith in Christ, passed gradually, and, in different countries, more or less rapidly, though with comparative silence, into infant baptism in the more modern sense, the baptism of new-born babes. For the most part, historical light in regard to the primitive churches shone but dimly. It is not strange if even the acute and powerful Augustine sometimes had his vision obscured in the heat and dust of controversy. We are not at all surprised at the manner in which he, in the fifth century, used the word *parvulus;* while, with consummate skill and energy, he confirmed and made triumphant in Africa and elsewhere that system of *infant* baptism which, according to the most reliable evidence, began to be authoritatively established in that country, by the ardent and popular Cyprian, about the middle of the third century.

But on those influences to which we have alluded we cannot now expatiate. Nor can we exhibit here the statements respecting baptism that are found in the works of those Fathers who preceded Origen. Not one of them says any thing in favor of infant baptism; while several of them speak in a manner that is quite inconsistent with the supposition of its having yet come into existence. For satisfactory information on this point, we can, with much confidence, refer our readers to an excellent article by the Rev. Dr. Ripley, in the Christian Review, for October, 1851.

In this connection, however, we may perhaps be permitted to add a very few words respecting Tertullian, who, about A.D. 200, in most decided tones of disapprobation, raises his voice against hastening the baptism of children.* He uses the very word that is used in the translations from Origen; and, in the course of his expostulation, he remarks: "The Lord does indeed say, *Forbid them not to come unto me.* Therefore let them come while they are growing up; let them come while they are learning, while they are being taught whither they are coming. Let them be made Christians [be identified by baptism with the body of Christians] when they shall have been able to know Christ."†

* Præcipuè circa parvulos.

† Ait quidem Dominus, *nolite illos prohibere ad me venire.*

In order to be able to know Christ, they needed not only a mind adapted to perceive, but they needed also to have Christ presented to the mind. They needed skillful and patient guidance; as, when Philip asked, Understandest thou what thou readest? the eunuch replied, How can I, except some man guide me? It is not when they merely begin to be susceptible of this knowledge, but when by means of sufficient age, and of suitably extended instruction, they may reasonably be supposed to be acquainted with the character and religion of our Lord, that Tertullian would have children baptized. He objects only to such haste as would preclude their being duly instructed and established in the principles of piety. He would have them come to Christ by being carefully taught, and receiving the Christian religion. Hence it would seem that he was speaking, not of babes or infants properly so called, but of such children as were, at least in some measure, capable of being taught.

To the same conclusion the Chevalier Bunsen was conducted by his investigations, the results of which he has recently given to the world in his very learned work, entitled, "Hippolytus and his Age." The opinion is there stated most decidedly, in the following terms: "Tertullian's opposition is to the

---

Veniant ergo dum adolescunt, veniant dum discunt, dum quo veniant docentur; fiant Christiani quum Christum nosse potuerint. *Lib. De Baptismo*, c. 18.

baptism of young, growing children ; he does not say a word about new-born infants. Neither does Origen, when his expressions are accurately weighed."*

We commend the subject to the consideration of our readers. We have endeavored to call forth Origen himself, as it were, and let him give his own testimony. This has been uttered in his own language, the Greek, as well as in a translation, so far as it respects the principal passages and several of the others. No room is left for suspicion of fraud, or spuriousness. If we have fallen into error at any point, may we be set right. If passages which have commonly been supposed to favor infant baptism, have been satisfactorily reconciled by us with passages which decidedly exclude it, all is well. But if this has not been done, and a passage existing only in a translation, or liable to some suspicion of spuriousness, is at variance with a passage existing still in the original Greek, or liable to no such suspicion, it is clear that preference must be given to the authority of the passage still existing in the original, or liable to no suspicion. The conclusion is easy and inevitable. *Origen should never be quoted in support of infant baptism.* He testifies, not only indirectly but also directly and expressly in regard to children as well as others, that, before being baptized, they were to be taught, and to give evidence of having duly heeded the voice of Christian instruction.

* Vol. iii., p. 195.

BAPTISM FOR THE DEAD.

BAPTISM FOR THE DEAD.

WHAT was it to be baptized for the dead, as mentioned in 1 Cor. xv : 29?

We confess that we are not prepared to acquiesce in the conclusion to which Conybeare and Howson come, in their elaborate and excellent work on the Life and Epistles of St. Paul, namely, that "the passage must be considered to admit of no satisfactory explanation. It alludes to some practice of the Corinthians, which has not been recorded elsewhere, and of which every other trace has perished."* We think that Dr. Kendrick has sufficiently shown the unsatisfactory character of that explanation which has been sought in supposing that the apostle Paul referred to the superstitious baptism of living persons instead of some who had died unbaptized. We doubt the correctness of the interpretation given by Doddridge, Olshausen and others, that "baptized *for* (ὑπὲρ) is baptized *instead of* the dead, to fill up the ranks vacated by the dead; to replace those whom death has snatched away." And we have not been con-

* Vol. II., p. 63.

vinced by the logic and eloquence recently employed in maintaining that "*Baptized for the dead* is baptized into a relation to the dead, baptized so as to be allied with the dead, reckoned among the dead rather than among the living; so baptized as that they belong, by sacrifice, suffering, peril, martyrdom, rather to the dead than to the living, and are thus the victims of a fate which has no alleviation nor apology, except in the resurrection."

Without attempting to discuss the merits of the numerous opinions which have been brought forward respecting the passage before us, we would call attention to a few considerations, in the hope that they may help some candid and inquiring reader to understand the meaning of the apostle.

It is undeniable that the word in the Greek original (ὑπὲρ) corresponding to *for* in the phrase "baptized for the dead," is used, in the New Testament and in the Greek classics, to signify not only *instead* or *in the place of*, but also *respecting* or *with reference to*—and *for*, modified in various ways by the context; as to die, suffer, make an offering, hope, thank, speak, pray, contend, support the claims set up *for*, etc. The following passages may serve as illustrations: 2 Cor. xii: 8, For (ὑπὲρ, *respecting*) this thing I besought the Lord that it might depart from me. 2 Cor. xii: 8, We would not, brethren, have you ignorant of (ὑπὲρ, *respecting* or *with reference to*) our trouble. 2 Thess. ii: 1, Now we beseech you, brethren, by (ὑπέρ, *concerning* or *with respect to*) the coming of our Lord Jesus Christ. Phil. i: 7, It is meet for me to think this of (ὑπὲρ, *with reference to*) you all. 2 Cor. i: 7, Our hope of (ὑπὲρ, *respecting* and *for*) you is steadfast. Rom. i: 8, I thank my God through Jesus Christ for (ὑπὲρ, *with reference* or *regard to*) you all, that your faith is spoken of throughout the whole world. Acts xxvi: 1, Then Agrippa said unto Paul, Thou art permitted to speak for (ὑπὲρ) thyself. The apostle was permitted to state what he deemed to be the facts in his case, and thus show why he should not be condemned. So among the Greeks, "to speak *for* the commonwealth" (ὑπὲρ τοῦ κοινοῦ) was to "defend it." Compare the expression, If for us (ὑπὲρ ἡμῶν, nostra causa) you shall not be able to *act* (πράττειν) as sustaining our interests.* According to Xenophon's account in the preceding part of the paragraph, it will be recollected, Cyrus had said that he was not able to *speak*, that is, to set forth for his companions, before the proper authority, the claims of the petition which was to be presented; and his companions had asked, Who would be more capable of *persuading?* A kindred expression occurs in the next book, If I counsel Cyrus to say something for us (τι εἰπεῖν ὑπὲρ ἡμῶν.)†

The Greek preposition of which we are speaking indicates, most usually, that the act mentioned in connection with it, whether external or internal, has a favorable bearing, or is, in some way, on the side or

* Cyropedia, B. I: 6. † Cyropedia, B. II: 1.

in behalf of the object whose relation to the act it shows. Sometimes, as we have seen, it signifies merely *respecting* or *with reference to;* and then it is merely equivalent to the word περὶ, which usually has this signification. Sometimes the two words alternate; as in Eph. vi: 18 and 19, With all perseverance and supplication for (περὶ) all the saints; and for (ὑπὲρ) me, that utterance may be given unto me, etc. In the first case, the supplication requested is expressly *with respect to;* and impliedly, from the context and the nature of the act, it is *for.* In the second case, it is expressly *for;* and, of course, as the context also shows, it is *with respect to.* An equally clear instance of the alternation of these Greek prepositions, and of their being used as if equivalent to each other, may be found in the seventh chapter of the second book of Maccabees. In the ninth verse, one of the seven sons who, with their mother, was put to death by Antiochus Epiphanes, says, "the King of the world shall raise us up unto everlasting life who have died for (ὑπὲρ) his laws;" and in the thirty-seventh verse of the same chapter, another says, "I, as my brothers, offer up my body and life for (περὶ) the laws," etc. Those martyrs, by their sufferings, bore a noble testimony in behalf of the divine laws which the persecuting tyrant required them to disregard. Winer's careful statement should be remembered: "As among the Greeks, so in the New Testament, the two prepositions are interchanged with each other. (See Gal. i: 4.) And the writers themselves do not hold fast the difference. The combination of the two, however, is suitably presented in 1 Pet. iii. 18."*

Our Saviour, in discoursing with his disciples, brings very distinctly to view the idea of a great contest between two parties, the Christian and the Anti-Christian. In Luke ix: 50, he says, He that is not against us is for us (ὑπὲρ ἡμῶν); and in the parallel place of Mark ix: 40, He that is not against us is on our part (ὑπὲρ ἡμῶν). In both of these passages, as well as in 1 Cor. xv: 29 (for the dead, ὑπὲρ τῶν νεκρῶν), the author of the ancient Syriac version uses the same word that he does in Mark i: 44, and Luke v: 14, " Show thyself to the priests, and offer an oblation for thy cleansing." But in these last two passages the Greek word in the original corresponding to the one which he uses and to the English *for*, is the preposition (περὶ) which we have mentioned as more usually signifying *with reference to.* The offering was to be with reference to the cleansing. It was also to be a testimony for it, affirming with respect to it what was claimed in behalf of the leper, namely, the reality of his being cleansed or healed.

After the resurrection of Christ, as well as before it, he and his followers were on one side, while the unbelieving and scoffing world was on the other, in

* See the work entitled Grammatik des neutestamentlichen Sprachidioms, als Grundlage der neutestamentlichen Exegese, p. 328.

the great contest to which he referred when he said, He that is not against us is on our part, or for us (ὑπὲρ ἡμῶν). The claims that were set up for him and for those who trusted in him were rejected. His resurrection was denied, and all their hopes of resurrection and immortality were treated as delusive dreams.

If now it was understood that in the act of baptism there was a confiding reference to Christ's dying and rising again to deliver his followers from sin and death, they who were baptized did, in that act, take part with him and his friends. In being baptized they professed not only their trust in him and their devotedness to him as their Lord and Saviour, but also their belief in the rightfulness of all his claims, and in the timely fulfillment of all his gracious promises to his followers. What though some of these had gone down to the grave? He was able to raise them up again; for he himself had triumphed over death, and had ascended to "the right hand of the Majesty on high."

In reply to the objection that "water baptism is performed not *for* Christ (ὑπὲρ Χριστοῦ) but *into* Christ (εἰς Χριστὸν); we think it sufficient to remark that, while Christian baptism was always to recognize Christ as preached in the gospel, it might well be connected with some variety of expression, according to the various aspects in which that recognition is presented, or the various purposes for which it is mentioned. In the general commission given by our

Lord to his apostles, he speaks of baptizing disciples in or unto (εἰς) the name, that is, into the recognition of the Father, and of the Son, and of the Holy Spirit (Matt. xxviii: 19). And yet the apostles sometimes baptized into Christ Jesus (Rom. vi: 3, and Gal. iii: 27), or into the name of the Lord Jesus (Acts viii: 16, and xix: 5); sometimes baptized in or upon (ἐπί) the name of Jesus Christ (Acts ii: 38), the baptism being grounded upon the sincere and devout profession of faith in him; and sometimes, in a very similar sense, baptized in (ἐν) the name of the Lord (Acts x: 48). They had occasion to make Christ the prominent subject of their discourses; and if he was duly acknowledged, they could expatiate, at their discretion, on all contained in the commission and in the teaching of our Lord. At one time, they could refer to baptism as a suitable acknowledgment of Christ, who died on account of our sins, and thence proceed to remind us of our obligation to die to all sin, and rise to a new life, as he rose from the dead. At another time they could refer to baptism as a testimony borne for Christ and his departed followers, amidst the reproaches of that scoffing unbelief which denounced him as an impostor, and his followers as contemptible dupes, any resurrection being an impossibility. In the first case, they would contemplate us as receiving the Saviour; in the second as taking his part and testifying for him.

Christ had predicted his own resurrection. He had also declared, He that believeth on me, though he were dead, yet shall he live.* This is the will of Him that sent me, that every one who seeth the Son and believeth on him may have everlasting life; and I will raise him up at the last day.† And he had taught that the hour was coming in which all that are in the graves shall hear his voice, and shall come forth.‡ His own resurrection had divinely confirmed the authority of his mission on earth and the truth of all that he had taught. If he had risen, a resurrection was possible. What had been done could be done again. If he had risen, it was through an exertion of divine power. The same power can raise others. If he had risen, through an exertion of divine power, thus confirming his claims to be an unerring guide, then others will be raised up according to his prediction.

The apostle Paul regarded the defending of the claims set up for Christ as virtually the defending of "the hope and resurrection of the dead." In his address before the Jewish council at Jerusalem (Acts xxiii: 6), he is represented as saying, "Of the hope and resurrection of the dead I am called in question." In Acts xvii: 3, he is represented as "opening and alleging that Christ must needs have suffered, and risen from the dead." And in the 18th verse, which mentions his interview with "certain philosophers of the Epicureans and of the Stoics," is it stated that

* John xi: 25. † John vi: 40.
‡ John v: 28 and 29.

"he preached unto them Jesus and the resurrection." Respecting Peter and John it is recorded in Acts iv: 2, that they "taught the people, and preached through Jesus the resurrection from the dead." In Acts iv: 33, we have the summary statement, "With great power gave the apostles witness of the resurrection of the Lord Jesus." In Acts v: 30–32, they say, "The God of our fathers raised up Jesus, whom ye slew and hanged on a tree. Him hath God exalted with his right hand to be a Prince and a Saviour, for to give repentance to Israel and forgiveness of sins. And we are his witnesses of these things; and so is also the Holy Spirit, whom God hath given to them that obey him." In Acts x: 39–43, "And we are witnesses of all things which he did both in the land of the Jews and in Jerusalem, whom they slew and hanged on a tree. Him God raised up the third day, and showed him openly; not to all the people, but unto witnesses, chosen before of God, even to us who did eat and drink with him after he rose from the dead. And he commanded us to preach unto the people, and to testify that it is he who was ordained of God to be the Judge of quick and dead."

In Acts xiii: 28–39; we have a striking specimen of the manner in which Paul was accustomed to connect the death and the resurrection of Christ. He is addressing the Jews in the synagogue at Antioch in Pisidia; and he proceeds to say, "Though they found no cause of death in him, yet desired they Pilate that he should be slain. And when they had fulfilled all that was written of him, they took him down from the tree, and laid him in a sepulchre. But God raised him from the dead. And he was seen many days of them who came up with him from Galilee to Jerusalem, who are his witnesses unto the people. And we declare unto you glad tidings, how that the promise which was made unto the fathers, God hath fulfilled the same unto us their children, in that he hath raised up Jesus again; as it is also written in the second Psalm, Thou art my Son, this day have I begotten thee. And as concerning that he raised him up from the dead, now no more to return to corruption, he said on this wise: I will give you the sure mercies of David. Wherefore he saith also in another Psalm, Thou shalt not suffer thy Holy One to see corruption. For David, after he had served his own generation by the will of God, fell asleep, and was laid unto his fathers, and saw corruption. But he whom God raised again, saw no corruption. Be it known unto you, therefore, men and brethren, that through this man is preached unto you the forgiveness of sins; and by him all that believe are justified from all things, from which ye could not be justified by the law of Moses."

In his First Epistle to the Corinthians (xv: 3 and 4) he says: "I delivered unto you first of all, that which I also received, how that Christ died for our sins, according to the Scriptures, and that he was buried, and that he rose again the third day, according to the Scriptures, and that he was seen," etc. In his Epistle to the Romans (iv : 24 and 25) : "For us also to whom it shall be imputed, if we believe on him that raised up Jesus our Lord from the dead; who was delivered for our offences, and was raised again for our justification ;" and (x: 9 and 10) "the word of faith which we preach, that if thou shalt confess with thy mouth the Lord Jesus, and shalt believe in thy heart that God hath raised him from the dead, thou shalt be saved." In Rom. v : 10 : "If when we were enemies, we were reconciled to God by the death of his Son, much more, being reconciled, we shall be saved by his life." And viii : 34 : "Who is he that condemneth ? It is Christ that died; yea, rather, that is risen again, who is even at the right hand of God, who also maketh intercession for us. In his Epistle to the Philippians (iii : 20 and 21) : "From whence also we look for the Saviour, the Lord Jesus Christ; who shall change our vile body, that it may be fashioned like unto his glorious body, according to the working whereby he is able even to subdue all things unto himself." In Rom. viii: 23, looking forward to the glory which shall be revealed in us, he mentions, as a completing portion of it, *the redemption of our body.* He consoles the bereaved disciples at Thessalonica (1 Thess. iv: 13 and 14), by saying: "I would not have you to be ignorant, brethren, concerning them who are asleep, that ye sorrow not, even as others who have no hope. For if [or as] we be lieve that Jesus died and rose again, even so them also who sleep in Jesus will God bring with him."

The same apostle, standing on Mars' Hill, closes his address to the men of Athens by saying: "The times of this ignorance God winked at, but now commandeth all men everywhere to repent; because he hath appointed a day in which he will judge the world in righteousness, by that man whom he hath ordained; whereof he hath given assurance unto all, in that he hath raised him from the dead."

And, in harmony with these representations, the apostle Peter, in his First Epistle (i: 3 and 4) renders thanks to God, "who, according to his abundant mercy, hath begotten us again unto a lively hope by the resurrection of Jesus Christ from the dead, to an inheritance incorruptible, and undefiled, and that fadeth not away."

These, and other passages that we pass over in silence, indicate the importance which the apostles attached to the resurrection of Christ. It puts the impress of the divine sanction on all his claims; and it is indissolubly connected with the state and prospects of his followers. Hence, the resurrection was regarded as a primary fact in the Christian system. It is mentioned in the Epistle to the Hebrews (vi: 1 and 2) as being one of the elementary teachings, one of *the principles of the doctrine of Christ.*

Our Saviour had said, *I am the resurrection and the*

*life.** He is the source of our new life, spiritual and moral, with the well founded hope that he will finally redeem even our bodies, making them "spiritual" (1 Cor. xv : 44), "like unto his glorious body," fitted for the heavenly state, and will give us, in our completed redemption, to enjoy with him eternal bliss. He died on account of our sins. We die or become dead to sins. He rises from the dead to a glorious and eternal life. We rise by faith in him to a new spiritual and moral life, which is connected with a glorious resurrection hereafter, even of the body, and with the life everlasting in the heavenly mansions. Our deadness to sin and our new life, our rising to holiness here, with the hope of a happy future resurrection, and the enjoyment of the eternal bliss promised by the Saviour, we owe, pre-eminently, to his death and resurrection. His death is the procuring cause; his resurrection, the crowning assurance.

According to our Lord's command, whoever trusted in him for salvation was to be baptized. Baptism was indeed a symbol of purification; for it was performed in water, a purifying element. And, at the same time, it indicated the source of the purification. In 1 John i : 7, it is affirmed that the blood of Jesus Christ . . . cleanseth us from all sin. And in Rev. i : 5, glory and dominion forever and ever are ascribed unto him that loved us, and washed us from our sins in his own blood. It is to Christ, suffering a

* John xi : 25.

bloody and ignominous death for us, and, as he predicted, rising gloriously from the tomb, that we are to look, with penitence and faith, for purification from our sins, and for resurrection to a life holy and faithful here, glorious hereafter, and completely happy forever. Christian baptism, therefore, when the apostles were fully illuminated, was perceived to have an important and impressive reference to the death of Christ.

In the view of the Saviour, even before his crucifixion, his sufferings and death appeared as a baptism. He was to be overwhelmed, as it were, in deep waters; and yet he was to rise again, gloriously triumphant. "I have a baptism," he said, "to be baptized with; and how am I straitened till it be accomplished."*

Respecting the import of that simple and solemn rite which he appointed to be observed, in the outset, by all who profess faith in him, we can have no guides more reliable than his own apostles. One of these (in the First Epistle of Peter iii: 20 and 21), mentions the rescue of those who in the ark were raised up through the waters of the flood, as resembling our being saved amidst the solemnities of baptism, not a mere external washing, but the seeking or professing of a good conscience towards God, *through the resurrection of Jesus Christ.* Here, it will be perceived, he connects our *baptism* with the

* Luke xii: 50.

resurrection of Christ, and, of course, with his death; for his death is necessarily presupposed in the mention of his resurrection.

Another apostle connects our baptism expressly with the *death* of Christ. In Rom. vi: 3, he mentions our baptism as manifestly recognizing that death. Presuming that the matter was distinctly understood by every one who had been baptized, he asks, *Know ye not that so many of us as were baptized into Jesus Christ, were baptized into his death?* This apostle also connects our baptism with the *resurrection* of Christ. For he immediately adds, "Therefore we are buried with him by baptism into death [and, of course, raised up again], *that, like as Christ was raised up from the dead* by the glory of the Father, even so we also should walk in newness of life. For if we have been planted together—united with him—in the likeness of his death, we shall be also in the likeness of his resurrection . . . . If we be dead with Christ, we believe that we shall also live with him."

In regard to the words which we have here inserted in brackets, namely: *and, of course, raised up again*, it must be evident to every attentive reader that they are suggested and required by the context. And this is confirmed by the parallel passage in the Epistle to the Colossians (ii: 12), where both the being buried with Christ and the being risen or raised up with him, are fully expressed, as pertaining to the baptismal act: "Buried with him *in baptism*, *wherein* [in which emblem] *also* ye are risen with him through the faith of the operation of God, who hath raised him from the dead."

In conversation and in writing, we often omit words and clauses, as being implied by the expressions used, especially when those expressions, from the nature of the things mentioned, or from frequent usage, have come to suggest readily all that needs to be presented to the mind. We are informed respecting Naaman the Syrian (2 Kings v : 14), "Then went he down and dipped himself seven times in Jordan." We do not need to have it expressed that he rose up again as often as he dipped himself; this is implied. When the mariner who was once approaching some unknown or dangerous coast, tells us that, to ascertain the depth of the water, he threw the lead, and for many hours continued to throw it, that is, to sink the plummet for sounding at sea; every one who has any knowledge of the process readily understands that as often as he threw and sank the lead he raised it up again. And when we speak of immersion as a religious rite, we assume it, as a matter of course, that the person immersed is raised up again. The nature of the case speaks for itself. And in every mind the rising again, whether expressed or implied, is connected with the immersion. Otherwise, this would be a drowning. But as no one suspects us of having any intention to commit such a crime, and as our practice of raising up again those whom we bury in baptism is well known, a single word is sufficient to present to the view of the mind the whole emblematical act.

In the explanation of these passages we do not stand alone. To say nothing of many others, whose opinions are entitled to a respectful regard, we request our readers to remember that, with reference to the passage in Rom. vi : 4, Conybeare and Howson have the candor to remark,* "This clause, which is here left elliptical, is fully expressed, Col. ii : 12, συνταφέντες αὐτῷ ἐν τῷ βαπτίσματι ἐν ᾧ καὶ συνηγέρθητε. This passage cannot be understood unless it be borne in mind that the primitive baptism was by immersion." See Vol. I., p. 439.

Before closing this article, we may have occasion to advert to what is there stated.

We now hasten to bring together the elements of a solution of the problem before us. These, we think, are to be found in the context, and on the face of the verse itself, 1 Cor. xv : 29, which we are endeavoring to explain.

In the context preceding, the apostle speaks of Christ's death for us, of his burial, and of his resurrection, proved by the testimony of eye-witnesses, of all the apostles, and of more than five hundred brethren at once. These facts. he represents as having been most prominent in his preaching, So, he says, we preach, and so ye believed. Now, he asks, "If Christ be preached that he rose from the dead, how

* Vol. II., p. 169.

say some among you, that there is no resurrection of the dead?"

Here follows an expostulation, showing the unreasonableness and the pernicious consequences of such a rejection of the truth. If there be no resurrection, then (1) Christ is not risen; (2) the preaching of the apostles and the faith of their disciples are useless; (3) the apostles testify falsely respecting Christ's resurrection; (4) the whole gospel is a delusive fable, and brings no deliverance from sin; (5) they who have died trusting in Christ have perished; (6) we too are in a most miserable condition, for our most splendid hope of a glorious immorality, for which we forego every thing else, perishes when we die.

Here, in contrast with so unutterably miserable a disappointment to the followers of Christ, there is brought to view a glimpse of the happy consequences of his resurrection, his triumphing over all enemies, even over death itself, and completing gloriously his mediatorial work.

Having thus digressed a little according to his glowing manner, the apostle reverts, in the 29th verse, to the train of his expostulations: (7) "Else, what shall they do that are baptized for the dead, if the dead rise not at all? Why are they baptized for the dead?" As much as to say, How, if there be no resurrection, can they escape the charge of inconsistency, or of falsehood, who, in most solemnly professing their faith, are immersed or buried in baptism and raised up again, with reference to the dead, as if testifying for them, that their resurrection ought to be regarded as a fundamental truth? Why do they exhibit this testimony, this emblematical act with reference to the dead? That is, with reference pre-eminently to Christ, who, the gospel affirms, died for us and rose again, and then, consequently, with reference to others whose resurrection he foretold. (8) And why, confiding in Christ, as if he had risen from the dead, and thus taking part with him and his followers, do we stand forth before the world, exposed every hour to persecution and to death? Why do I, as it were, die daily? What am I to gain by all my conflicts and sufferings? I am bereft of reason and common sense. Beyond the grave, there is no crown of righteousness laid up for the faithful.—A conclusion so impious, in view of all the light that now shines on the subject, is instinctively rejected by every Christian heart; and the denial from which it comes must be pronounced to be a denial of the truth.

What is contained in number 7, leads very naturally to what is contained in number 8; but it is not identical with it. The difference seems to be this: in number 7, the question is, Why give such a testimony, so false or so inconsistent. And then, in number 8, Why, by giving that testimony, or by any other act, expose ourselves to persecution?

Our interpretation may be briefly expressed thus: The context treats of rising from the dead. To be baptized was to be immersed or "buried in baptism," and, of course, raised up again. And this was done with reference to the dead; so that, inasmuch as it was taking, decidedly, their part, the solemn emblematical act testified for them a belief in their resurrection. Christ rose from the dead, and all his followers must. Christ rose; and his followers are to rise to a life new and holy, though it may be persecuted and self-denying here, and to a life completely and forever glorious hereafter. Christ rose. He will come at the last day. The living and the dead will stand before him, and they will be judged in righteousness.

The conclusion to which we have come, it will be perceived, rests on a basis independent of the opinions, whether well founded or not, of men who have taught since the days of the apostles. But we may be permitted now to remark that it is confirmed, substantially, by early writers of the highest authority in the Greek Church; men whose native language was Greek, and who, in other respects also, had ample means of understanding the passage. They represent baptism as having reference to the death of Christ, and to a rising again. In so representing this initiatory rite, they sometimes, like Paul in Rom. vi: 4, mention only our immersion, our going under or being buried in the water, and leave our emerging or rising again to be understood as a matter of course. And sometimes, like Paul in Col. ii: 12, they mention both the burial and the rising.

The fact that they deemed it sufficient to mention the well known act in an elliptical manner, would strongly corroborate our explanation of Rom. vi: 4, if it needed to be corroborated.

Chrysostom, in his *Homily* xxiii., on the First Epistle to the Corinthians, uses the following expression: "We, when we have believed in Christ and his resurrection, are baptized."* In his *Homily* xl., on the same Epistle he says: "To be baptized and put under, then raised up, is an emblem of going down into the state of the dead, and of rising from it."† In the same connection he represents Paul as saying, "If there is not a resurrection, why art thou baptized for the dead? that is, the bodies. For upon this thou art baptized, believing in a resurrection of the dead body."‡

Theodoret says, "he that is baptized is buried with the Lord, that, taking part with him in his death, he may also be a partaker of his resurrection. But if the body is dead and does not rise, why then is it baptized?"§

John of Damascus, in his theological work on the

---

* . . . . ἡμεῖς τῷ Χριστῷ πιστεύσαντες καὶ τῇ ἀναστάσει αὐτοῦ βαπτιζόμεθα.

† Τὸ βαπτίζεσθαι καὶ καταδύεσθαι, εἶτα ἀνανεύειν, τῆς εἰς ᾅδου καταβάσεως ἐστι σύμβολον, καὶ τῆς ἐκεῖθεν ἀνόδου.

‡ Εἰ μή ἐστιν ἀνάστασις, τί καὶ βαπτίζῃ ὑπὲρ τῶν νεκρῶν; τουτέστι, τῶν σωμάτων. Καὶ γὰρ ἐπὶ τούτῳ βαπτίζῃ, τοῦ νεκροῦ σώματος ἀνάστασιν πιστεύων.

§ Ὁ βαπτιζόμενός, φησι, τῷ δεσπότῃ συνθάπτεται, ἵνα τοῦ θανάτου κοινωνήσας καὶ τῆς ἀναστάσεως γένηται κοινωνός. εἰ δὲ νεκρὸν ἐστι τὸ σῶμα, καὶ οὐκ ἀνίσταται, τί δήποτε καὶ βαπτίζεται.

Orthodox Faith, B. iv. c. 11, teaches that Baptism is an emblem of the death of Christ.*

Theophylact on Col. ii : 12, says : "He that is baptized is buried with Christ ;"† on Col. iii : 1, "as by the going under, baptism typifies death, so by the rising again, the resurrection ;"‡ and on 1 Cor. x : 2, "we ourselves are baptized, imitating death by going under, and the resurrection by the rising again."§

Whoever prepared the remarkable Greek work claiming to be the Apostolic Constitutions, aimed, doubtless, to make it seem, in his early time, to express the views of the apostles. And in B. iii. c. 17, he says :"This baptism therefore is given into the death of Jesus. The water is instead of the burial ; . . . . the descent into the water, the dying together with Christ ; the ascent out of the water, the rising again with him."||

And whatever may be the true history of that creed which, after a few ages, came to be ascribed to the apostles, and which contained, as one of the articles usually professed at baptism, the doctrine of *the*

---

* Τύπος τοῦ θανάτου τοῦ Χριστοῦ ἐστι τὸ βάπτισμα.

† Ὁ βαπτισθεὶς συνθάπτεται τῷ Χριστῷ.

‡ Τὸ βάπτισμα ὥσπερ διὰ τῆς καταδύσεως, θάνατον, οὕτω διὰ τῆς ἀναδύσεως, τὴν ἀνάστασιν τυποῖ.

§ Βαπτιζόμεθα καὶ αὐτοὶ, μιμούμενοι τὸν θάνατον διὰ τῆς καταδύσεως, καὶ τὴν ἀνάστασιν διὰ τῆς ἀναδύσεως.

|| Ἔστι τοίνυν τὸ μὲν βάπτισμα εἰς τὸν θάνατον τοῦ Ἰησοῦ διδόμενον, τὸ δὲ ὕδωρ ἀντὶ ταφῆς, ... ἡ κατάδυσις τὸ συναποθανεῖν, ἡ ἀνάδυσις τὸ συναναστῆναι.

resurrection of the dead, no one can doubt that the apostles preached that doctrine, and taught their disciples to acknowledge it, in connection with acknowledging that Christ died for us and rose again.

Clement of Rome, in his First Epistle to the Corinthians, says: "Let us consider, beloved, how the Lord continually shows us that there shall be a future resurrection; of which he has made our Lord Jesus Christ the first-fruits, raising him from the dead."*

In comparatively modern times, many not accustomed to the ideas prevalent among the Greek ecclesiastical fathers, seem to us to have perceived, in part, the true interpretation of the passage before us. With Melancthon, they represent those who are *baptized for the dead*, as *making profession concerning the dead* (*profitentes de mortuis*). And yet they seem, very naturally in their circumstances, to have overlooked one or two considerations belonging to the case. We allude particularly to the peculiar appropriateness of what is expressed, and of what is implied, in the word baptized, immersed, βαπτιζόμενοι, buried, and of course raised up again.†

---

* Κατανοήσωμεν, ἀγαπητοὶ, πῶς ὁ Δεσπότης ἐπιδείκνυται διηνεκῶς ἡμῖν τὴν μέλλουσαν ἀνάστασιν ἔσεσθαι, ἧς τὴν ἀπαρχὴν ἐποιήσατο τὸν Κύριον Ἰησοῦν Χριστὸν, ἐκ νεκρῶν ἀναστήσας. (XXIV., id Jacobson's Edition; XI: 16, in Wakefield's.)

† Since this article was written, we have had the pleasure of reading the following note in the English translation, at Edinburgh, of the sixth edition of Winer's

Dr. Meyer, pre-eminent in Germany and elsewhere at the present time among the learned interpreters of the New Testament, in the recent edition of his Commentary on the Acts of the Apostles, says, respecting the baptism of the jailer (Acts xvi : 23) : *The immersion, certainly, was an entirely essential part of the symbolical representation in baptism.* And, for confirmation of his remark, he refers to the sixth chapter of the Epistle to the Romans.*

In the work, which we have already mentioned, on the Life and Epistles of St. Paul, by two very highly esteemed clergymen of the Established Church of

---

Work on the New Testament Diction (p. 400). It is from the pen of the translator, Edward Masson, A.M., formerly Professor in the University of Athens. . . . . . .
"Baptism is administered *in reference to*, represents *the state of the dead*, physical and spiritual, and subsequent resurrection through Christ. Chrysostom (*Homily* xx. on John), says : *Τίς ὁ λόγος τοῦ βαπτίσματος; θεῖα τελεῖται ἐν αὐτῷ σύμβολα, τάφος καὶ νέκρωσις, καὶ ἀνάστασις καὶ ζωή. Καὶ ταῦτα ὁμοῦ γίνεται πάντα.* [What is the reason of baptism? There are celebrated in its sacred symbols, burial and death, and resurrection and life. And these all occur together.] The rite of Baptism, according to the Greeks, always comprehended *κατάδυσις* and *ἀνάδυσις*, the one representing death, and the other resurrection. The alleged usage in the apostolic Church, of baptizing the (literally) dead, directly or vicariously, would have been, had it really existed, what Calvin calls it, *foeda baptismi profanatio*." . . . .

* Das Untertauchen war ja ein ganz wesentliches Stück der Taufsymbolik. (Rom. vi.)

England, there is a paragraph to which, according to our intimation, we now advert. They are speaking on affairs pertaining to the churches in the time of the apostle, and they proceed thus: "It is needless to add, that baptism was (unless in exceptional cases) administered by immersion, the convert being plunged beneath the surface of the water to represent his death to the life of sin, and then raised from his momentary burial to represent his resurrection to the life of righteousness. It must be a subject of regret that the general discontinuance of this original form of baptism (though perhaps necessary in our northern climates) has rendered obscure to popular apprehensions, some very important passages of Scripture."*

No exceptional cases in the times of the apostles, we are confident, can be shown. Exceptional cases, in later times, arose from erroneously supposing the necessity of baptism in order to be saved, and from erroneously ascribing to such a ceremony a kind of magical efficacy in communicating divine grace.

With the exercise of a little taste and skill and common sense, such as our Lord had a right to expect in his ministers and his people, immersion can be decorously administered *in all the world.* In every habitable region of the earth, suitable arrangements for the ceremony can easily be made, with due regard to the habits of any age or country.

* Vol. I. p. 439.

In respect to our northern climates, it should be remembered that, during a part of the year, there was cold weather in Palestine, where our Lord instituted baptism. In Greece, too, and in the Russian Empire, there is cold weather. And yet, in Greece and throughout even the highest latitudes of the Russian Empire, and wherever the Greek Church has prevailed, the Greek word baptism, βάπτισμα, has been understood to signify and require immersion; and immersion is continued to the present day. In our own country, and in the presence of numerous spectators, at Nahant and Newport and other places where there is "much water," we find it practicable to enjoy the salutary effect and the luxury of bathing And can it be impracticable for us to be baptized according to the original institute of our Lord and Saviour? If at any time it be so, and if we really seek to obey him, he, doubtless, will be well pleased with our waiting, reverently and confidingly, till it be practicable. Can it, then, be necessary, and can it be right, to discontinue the use of that symbolical or emblematical act which he himself, in his wisdom and love, appointed; and which sets forth so impressively a profession of dying to all sin and living to righteousness, through a faith in him who was dead, and is alive, and will hereafter raise up his followers to a completely glorious immortality?

www.ingramcontent.com/pod-product-compliance
Lightning Source LLC
LaVergne TN
LVHW010234110826
845151LV00004B/1292

* 9 7 8 1 4 2 5 5 2 4 5 1 7 *